Blind Devotion

Enhancing the Lives of Blind and Visually Impaired Dogs

Cathy Symons CVT CCRP

CONTENTS

FOR TOM, BOODA, CHOPPER AND DIGGER

Disclaimer

The contents contained in this book are for information purposes only, and may not apply to your situation. The author, publisher, distributor and provider provide no warranty about the content or accuracy of content enclosed. Information provided is subjective. Opinions expressed are that of the author. Keep this in mind when reviewing this guide. The author is not responsible or liable for injury, misinterpretation, or misuse of material. This text is not a substitute for seeking professional veterinary care. Endorsements of any products are strictly the opinion of the author. Products are meant as examples. The author accepts no liability for injury or misuse of products. The author received no monetary compensation for product endorsement.

INTRODUCTION

From a young age, I have had an innate love and respect for all living things. For me working with animals has always been a calling. I am a veterinary technician and have been caring for animals for over 25 years. I started my career in 1986 at the Angell Animal Medical Center located in Boston Massachusetts. I worked in the Radiology Department where I became the Assistant Supervisor of the Radiology and Nuclear Medicine Department. During my time there, I developed training manuals, educated incoming students, preformed routine radiographs and assisted with procedure such as; the placement of pacemakers, and conducting ultrasounds.

I left Angell in January of 1993 to work for Doctor Marge McMillan at The Windhover Veterinary Center as the head technician. In the beginning, Windhover was primarily a practice that specialized in birds, and I was thrilled with the new challenge. With my background in radiology I began teaching basic avian radiology techniques to students, other veterinary technicians, and veterinarians.

Over time Windhover grew and expanded its client base. Doctor McMillan is a board-certified radiologist, and her practice attracted patients with mobility problems. Some of these problems could be surgically corrected and some could not. From my perspective, some patients, took a long time to heal from surgery and there was little to be offered to the geriatric patients with osteoarthritis. My own dog was born with a degenerative condition of the hip that required surgical repair. It was these cases, along with my own dog's needs, that made me aware of the need for physical rehabilitation in veterinary medicine.

I began my course work at the University of Tennessee in canine rehabilitation in 2002 and in June of 2003, I became one of the first 36 people in the country to become a Certified Canine Rehabilitation Practitioner (CCRP). The same year, I was instrumental in establishing one of the first veterinary rehabilitation centers in Massachusetts. I now manage the rehabilitation program at The Sterling Impression Animal Rehabilitation Center. Much of my professional life is devoted to teaching students who are interested in pursuing a career in veterinary rehabilitation. Veterinarians, physical therapists and veterinary technicians come from all over the country to intern at The Sterling Impression Animal Rehabilitation Center.

I could not have predicted that the knowledge and expertise I've gained as a Canine Rehabilitation Practitioner would come to play a crucial role in my personal life as well. I applied that knowledge and expertise to help my dog, Booda, regain his quality of life following the loss of his eyesight.

Booda was the incredible canine creature I had the great honor of living with for 14 years. Two weeks after my husband and I were married, a twelve-week old pug joined our family, and it was always the three of us after that. Who would have thought our lives could have been so completely controlled by a pug? Booda was full of self-confidence and self-love. Even as a puppy his walks would turn to a strut, with his head up, chest out and tail pulled tightly onto his back when he realized he was being watched. We believed him to be perfect, and everything that he did was brilliant. It wasn't just us, as our families were smitten with him too. My colleagues at work would cater to his every wish. With this combination of nature and nurture, he began to believe he was someone quite special and should be treated as such, hence his nickname, "The Emperor."

Each day I eagerly looked forward to arriving home so I can be greeted by him and see his curly cinnamon bun tail wag feverishly. Sometimes, when I was out I would remember that he is at home and I get happy and giggly just thinking of him. He helped me to put my worries aside and reminded me what joy was every day. I learned many lessons from him; how to be a better human being, how to laugh at myself, how to live in the moment. Speak up when I'm not happy, be clear about my needs, and be loyal, honest and kind. Most importantly, to love who you are.

In turn, it brought me great despair when Booda became ill. In his short lifetime he had many medical problems and I spent many sleepless nights on the floor caring for him. I never thought that I could be so affected by a dog. When he started to have eye problems I had to put medicine in his eye every two hours throughout the day and night. His needs increased greatly when he became sick and he relied on me for his care.

My experience with Booda gave me a valuable perspective into the human animal bond and I feel I am better able to understand our patients and their humans because of this. These experiences made me a better technician, a better rehabilitation practitioner and a better human being. I am able to empathize more deeply with clients and have a better understanding of their pet's needs and the owner's concerns. The amazing thing is that through most of his medical conditions Booda's enthusiasm for life and his self-love could not be squelched.

At seven years old Booda went blind in his right eye. Just as he was learning to compensate for this loss, we learned the devastating news that he was going blind in his left eye too. In a matter of months, he was completely blind and would need to have his right eye removed. His newfound blindness imposed a threat to his confidence and his spirit. Not only did we have to help Booda find a way to regain his lifestyle, but we also had to help him overcome his fears so that he could find his way back to being the happy and well-adjusted dog we all knew he was at his core.

There are many things that we as owners can do to make sure our blind companions maintain a happy and interesting lifestyle. Effectively sustaining our pet's psychological health is imperative, which is primarily done through building a close relationship based on a strong sense of trust. Through environmental enrichment with social interaction, play, positive training, and mental stimulation, our dogs can learn to regain trust in their own instincts and surroundings, with us as their guide.

Through sharing our story, I hope to offer other pet owners reassurance, guidance, and motivation, all while sharing ideas and inspiring hope.

Booda's Story

I have always been drawn to animals and for as long as I can remember; I have wanted a dog, which I couldn't have as a child. My brother was extremely frightened of dogs so having a dog really was out of the question. However, we did have cats, four to be exact. Even then I was amazed how central they were to our lives. All of my family loved those cats. They have been gone now for almost 15 years but we still talk about them. They really brought us together as a family.

As a single adult, my lifestyle just wouldn't allow for living with a dog. I lived in a small apartment, I had two jobs and was going to school. I also had a boyfriend. Tom and I had been together for four years and were engaged to be married, but Tom wasn't really an animal person, at least not in the sense that I was. He had a dog growing up but he never really spoke passionately about it and the dog was really not central to the family. I, on the other hand, felt deeply passionate about having a dog, a desire that had been growing since childhood. As a child I dreamed about what it would be like to have a dog, having a constant companion, a friend, someone to confide in. As an adult I thought about hiking and running on the beach, doing agility and joining our friends at the dog park. It makes me laugh now because anyone who knows me knows I have never hiked and I hate the beach. Of course, in my fantasy I never had to pick up poop or clean smelly pug wrinkles.

I wanted what I considered a "real" dog. I was thinking maybe a Doberman Pincher. I had a childhood friend who had one. He was one of the sweetest and gentlest dogs I have ever met. My fantasies about having a dog were undeniably growing.

Finally, after all my fantasizing, I broached the topic. I told Tom I had always wanted to have a dog and how extremely important this was to me. We had bought a house and were two months away from getting married, so I thought this was the perfect time for me to have a dog. I wasn't sure how this would go over with Tom; after all, having a dog is a huge commitment. He said he needed some time to think this through. He approached me about it several days later. I could tell he had been putting a lot of thought into it. "Don't laugh," he was serious, "I want a pug."

I couldn't believe my ears. A pug? That's not a real dog. My only real experience with pugs was from work. They always seemed so emotional. They breathed weird and looked like an alien. Surely, I could never go hiking with a pug. My husband had a different view. He only knew one pug and she was extraordinary. He was always impressed with how happy she was all the time. She was gentle and sweet. She was an older dog who would sometimes stumble and fall, but that never seemed to bother her. She loved people and was always happy to see them. Sometimes she got so excited she fell over but she was always happy. Her owners made her a special bed with raised sides so she would not fall out. The other dogs in the family always wanted to get in there with her. Even though there was never enough room she allowed all of her pack mates to join her. Tom was really taken with her and her enthusiasm for life. That's the kind of dog he wanted.

My first response was, "I don't think a pug is going to be enough dog for me." This quote has come back to haunt me many times over from friends and family. Little did I know it was going to take a village to raise our pug.

I promised that I would seriously consider the pug and suggested we do some research to make sure this was the right dog for us. We had to be sure that a new dog would fit our lifestyle. We made a list of all of the traits that we wanted in a dog. We wanted a good family dog, a dog that would be good with children and other animals. We wanted a small dog but not a "foo foo" dog. We wanted a dog that would be hardy and tolerate moderate activity level. We did not want a dog that would challenge us too much. We wanted an easy dog, not necessarily a thinking dog; after all, this was our first dog. After all of our research, I had to admit Tom was right. We agreed the pug was a good choice for us. I found myself getting pretty excited about getting one.

A co-worker suggested that we pick out a breeder and look at some pug puppies. The breeder we chose mentioned that she had a litter of puppies. They were only a few weeks old but she had a light color male that she thought I would like. She mentioned that even though he was very young his personality was starting to develop and she thought he was feisty.

 I think I already knew this was going to be my dog. I thought about him every day and called every week to follow his progress.n Finally, the pups were old enough so we made the two-hour drive to New Hampshire to look at them. When we got there, it was chaos. There were pugs and puppies all running around. There was a lot of snorting and tail wagging. Everyone was trying to greet us all at once. I could barely focus on one dog or see my own feet.

The woman led us to two ten- week old male puppies. "He" was on the bottom of a two-pug pile snoring loudly and twitching slightly from dreaming. That was my puppy. My search was over; this was the dog I had waited my whole life for. He was absolutely adorable. He was fawn color with a black mask. He was wrinkly and fat, snorting softly when he sniffed you and spraying you with a fine mist when he exhaled. (a common experience amongst pug people) His brother was much darker in color with a pepper-color face. He was also very bossy. He took all the toys. He took all the treats. He tried to take all the attention. Our puppy was patient and tolerant, submitting to his brother's demands, seemingly oblivious or unconcerned about the situation. He was very endearing.

Tom thought it would be best if we took them outside and played with both puppies. He wanted to be sure this was the right dog for us. He was worried that he might be too shy, or too much of a push over. Wasted time in my opinion, I was in love. The great thing about our puppy was that he shined even more outside. When his brother would steal the toys he was playing with, he didn't care. When his brother tried to get all the attention, he didn't care. Whenever there was trouble he would stop, shake his body and move on with his life. A lesson I wish I could master. To seal the deal, he ran fast with no indication of breaking, head long into the back of my leg.

We never even looked at the other puppies. We put a deposit on him and set a date three weeks later to pick him up. It was difficult to leave him. We talked about him every day thereafter, even when we had to focus on the details of our wedding. For a wedding gift, my co-workers collected money to pay the breeder. It was the greatest gift ever.

We spent a week in Virginia for our honeymoon. Even though it was supposed to be a romantic trip, all I could think about was going home and getting our pug. While there, we visited pet stores to pick out new toys, collars, leashes, beds, coats, and anything a pug might need to make him comfortable. I remember the first toy I bought him; a plush hound dog. At the time the toy was actually bigger than he was and when he got it he would carry it around by its ears. I still have that toy and even though it is ragged and torn, it is one of my most valued possessions.

While shopping, we discovered a line of pet products called Booda® dog toys. We found this humorous since I thought that Booda actually looked like The Buddha, with his round face and a pot belly. We both thought this was a clever name. The spelling was changed to match the Booda® brand name which came with the name embroidered on all their toys.   From then on, he was Booda.

When we went to the breeder's house to pick him up, it was clear that he had grown in the short time we were away. He was now tall and gangly. A stage pug people refer to as the "uglies." Nothing about his body matched; his head was small, his legs were long, and his body was still round. I still loved him. The trip home was a little more traumatic than I had anticipated. On the two-hour ride home, he threw up, pooped and then peed in the car. Upon arriving home, he immediately explored every inch of the property and ate a dead cricket off the floor. I called one of our veterinarian friends asking where to take his batteries out. I should have seen his enthusiasm as a sign of things to come, but still we were pleased beyond reason. He was adorable.

The first two nights he cried a little but by the third night he had fallen fast and comfortably asleep. Even now I love to watch him sleep. There is nothing quite as relaxing to me as watching my pug sleep, watching the even rise and fall of his chest and listening to the sound of his snoring. Sometimes, while he was sleeping, he would stretch all the way out and then curl up both of his feet into little fists in front of his face. The first time I saw this sent me frantically looking for Tom so he wouldn't miss it. Every night we would play chase and there would be a mad dash around the house before passing out for the night.

We had done our research on pugs and all of it said pugs had a low to moderate activity level. Not so true. We could barely keep up with him. He never stopped. Once we caught him on the couch drinking soda out of a glass on the side table. As I started to run toward him, he started to drink faster, trying to take in as much as he could before I got to him. Then, to escape, he ran across the coffee table. It was hard to be mad at him, he was so proud of himself. Every day, he made me laugh.

Booda has always lived in the moment. He enjoyed everything. Walking Booda every night made fall my favorite time of year. Every time a leaf would fall he would jump it until the next leaf fell and he would jump that leaf and so it would go on leaf to leaf. Sometimes he would jump up to catch them as they were falling to the ground. Sometimes he would get down real low and stalk the leaves, quietly sneaking up on them and then move in for "the kill."

It was on these walks that I started to have a bizarre experience. I would be walking Booda and someone driving by in their car would yell out "Pug!" This happened on several occasions. It made me laugh. One day when crossing the street, a rather large man driving a trash truck stopped to let us cross. As I was crossing he blew his horn. Annoyed, I looked over at him, only to see him rolling down his window and yell "Pug!" It was at that moment I realized I belonged to an elite club of pug enthusiasts and the mere sight of a pug would cause people to lose their minds and scream out "Pug!"

Tom was overwhelmed with the amount of Booda's activity and he seemed to hold himself back. I think he was still trying to understand this active furry alien that was not quite how the pug books described. He would ask me "How do you two come up with so many games?"

Actually, Booda came up with all the games and it was natural for me to play along.

It didn't come so naturally to Tom. Amazingly, Booda's persistence eventually won Tom over. He loved Tom. Booda wanted to sit with him, walk with him, and play with him. He would spend time just gazing into Tom's face, as if he was examining every feature with great admiration. Whenever I sat next to Tom he would run from where ever he was to squeeze himself in-between us. I oscillated between a close second and a mere servant to his needs. It wasn't long before he had completely won Tom over. Though he had reeled in and had Tom fully secured, Booda still spent time simply admiring Tom.

It was time to start doing some training with Booda. After his first day of class it was suggested that Booda have "private" after class tutoring. I think they tried to put a positive spin on Booda having "private" after school lessons, but I knew what that meant. None of the other dogs had to stay after school. At first, I believed that it was because Booda was not a quick learner but it turns out that I was the problem. How humiliating! Booda performed beautifully for his trainer as if he had known these commands all of his life.

When I took control, you could see instant confusion. Booda would go through his whole routine- first sitting, then down, then giving his paw in hopes that one of those was what I wanted him to do. He had pulled out all his best stuff; what else could I possibly want?

I constantly made mistakes. I had worked with animals all of my life so, I just assumed this would come naturally for me, but it did not. I could not figure out how to get him to do what I wanted. I was completely stumped. I just could not grasp the concept of teaching him things like sit and down and stay. One of the things the trainer taught me was that Booda did not understand that Booda was a name, but was merely a command for getting him to make eye contact with me. She said, "What do you think he is thinking, I am Booda, I am Pug!?" Yes, I did. This was no ordinary pug. Perhaps she didn't know who she was dealing with.

Shortly after this event, he was given the nickname "The Emperor." Our training finally started to make sense to me when we started using a method called clicker training. Clicker training works by marking a desired behavior with a two-tone clicker. Any behavior can be marked, and once the dog understands the behavior, you can then give it a name, such as "sit." I finally had a way to communicate with Booda that worked for both of us.

Our lives with Booda started to fall into a comfortable routine. My favorite times were the evenings. The three of us would take a walk down the street for ice cream. It was such a peaceful event. We would eat our ice cream and Booda would chase the light from the flashlight all the way home. It became such a routine he would start looking for the beam of light before we turned the flashlight on. He would continuously scan the perimeter looking for the light and an opportunity to pounce on it. Booda would stand still and stalk it, with just his eyes moving back and forth, as if he could trick it into believing he wasn't watching it. This became one of his favorite games. When we wanted to tire him out, we would take him out in the yard, sit on the porch and train the flashlight back and forth.

It was during these walks that we started to notice signs of behavioural changes. Booda would sit down and rest more frequently. This was strange for Booda since, typically, he could barely contain his energy. On one occasion, he actually sat down and needed to be carried back. There were other signs. He would gather all of his toys in one spot to play with them, rather than chase after them. He was reluctant to run and sometimes would even cry while running. He was reluctant to lie all the way down and would keep his butt up in the air.

All of these things were strange in such a young dog. We took Booda to see our vet where, of course, he acted perfectly normal and showed no sign of pain. For the short term we were satisfied that it only happened occasionally and he was, for the most part, fine. Then, one day, he was playing chase with one of his best dog friends and screamed. I knew there was trouble. We x-rayed his hip that day. The diagnosis was Legg-Calves Perth's disease, or avascular necrosis, a hereditary disease that causes deterioration of the femoral head and neck, or the ball of the hip joint, due to a lack of blood supply.

It is more commonly seen in small breeds and it is typically treated by a surgical procedure to remove the ball of the hip. Once they remove the ball, scar tissue develops to form a "false" joint. The news was really hard to hear. Booda was only seven months old and needed orthopedic surgery. This was not what I thought having a dog was going to be like. I thought that because I was a veterinary technician, I could handle whatever might come our way as far as his health was concerned. The truth is I am just like every other dog owner. I have a deep emotional connection to my dog and I want to protect him and keep him safe. The hardest part of this was not being able to explain things to him. He trusted us completely and it broke my heart to see him struggle; I didn't want to violate that trust.

Booda was scheduled for the surgery. My husband and I both took the day off from work and set up camp in the office. I was amazed with Booda's bravery. He is so trusting of the doctors and staff at Windhover. They are like his family and I know that they all love him as much as he loves them. His relationship with our surgeon was a little bit more complicated. On one hand he was associated with some unpleasant things, but on the other hand he always carried cookies in his briefcase.

Booda came through surgery with flying colors. We wrapped him in warm towels, and listened to him snore. But I did wonder, "How do I protect him? How do I help him heal faster?"

That year I attended my first seminar on canine rehabilitation, and now my interest was sparked even more because I was helping my own dog recover from orthopedic surgery. I thought Booda was a great candidate for treatment. Although I was sad that my dog had needed orthopedic surgery, I was excited about the idea of putting my new skills to practice. I felt rejuvenated and was excited to learn more new things. I had learned how to preserve my dog's range of motion, along with some stretches and exercises to enhance his weight bearing and build muscle mass. I gathered all of my tools: hot packs for heating muscle, cold packs to cool him, a tape measure to measure his thigh girth. Trying to do rehab with Booda is like trying to hold onto a greased watermelon. For some unknown reason I thought it would be a good idea to videotape this glorious experience. It was twenty minutes of "get over here." "No! Put that down." "Get your head out of the trash." "What's in your mouth? Is that even food?"

It seemed as though Booda's enthusiasm for life had not been squelched. Still I wasn't discouraged. This was a good lesson for me when working in canine rehab, always have a plan B, and use what dogs like to do to your advantage. For Booda, I started to take him on some short leash walks, walking up hill to develop his back-leg muscles, and a little bit of controlled ball playing.   Booda's rehab was a great success it shortened his recovery time, increased his strength and endurance, and increased muscle development. He was back.

Booda and I had done so well together as a team, that I had the idea to enroll Booda in agility classes. Agility is a competition sport, where owners direct their dog through an obstacle course. An agility course might consist of going through tunnels, weaving around poles, jumping over bars, or running up a six foot "A" frame. Joining this class was about developing our relationship and having some fun. When I arrived, our classmates lined up for roll call and I saw the lineup. It went Border Collie, Border Collie,

Labrador, Border Collie, Pug. Booda was not the least bit embarrassed or intimidated. When The Emperor arrives people take notice.

Agility became something that we both very much enjoyed. It really changed our relationship. Booda became very in tune with subtle movements of my hands and shoulders. We could often predict each other's next moves. We really became quite a team. Booda became so good and he would get going so fast I couldn't get my commands out fast enough. It was sometimes embarrassing because he would scold me while on the field. It was clear he was reprimanding me for my unclear directions. Meanwhile my classmates are chanting his name "Boooooda! Boooooda! Boooooda!," perpetuating his already exaggerated feelings of superiority. The chanting and laughter fuelled Booda and he would take it upon himself to do "free-style" agility. (This is frowned upon as agility is supposed to be a controlled exercise.)

One of the more challenging obstacles in agility is the tunnel. The tunnel is essentially a long vinyl tube and can be shaped in a straight line or curved. The idea is to send your dog ahead of you and be at the end of the tunnel when they come out. Agility is also a competition of speed and accuracy and the owner can only use verbal commands or body signal to steer their dog in the right direction. You can't touch your dog and you can't touch the obstacles. When going through the tunnel the dog loses visual contact with their owner. Even though it's brief this can present a challenge when trying to convince a dog to go in.

My dog thought of the tunnel as more of a fort than an obstacle. I would send him ahead of me into the tunnel and run to the end and wait; no sign of pug. There were many occasions I would find myself crawling into the tunnel to drag him out. He would run in and not come out but you could see him peeking out the end. When I would come to get him, he would run to the other end and peek out. This would go on and on until I would crawl in on my hands and knees to drag him out. It would always send my classmates into roars of laughter. He slowly began taking over the class. He was a star and he was fearless. He became so disruptive that we would stand behind a wall to stop him from barking at the other dogs during their turn. This wall was eventually dubbed "The Wall of Shame." Booda and I often found ourselves behind it. Unfortunately, Booda feels no shame. I can only imagine what our lives would have been like if we had gotten the bossy pug.

Booda became so good at agility it was time to take our show on the road. We were asked by our dog club to perform an agility demonstration at the Boston Pet Expo. This would be fun and a great experience for both of us to get out in front of a crowd. We arrived early at our first agility demonstration and it was packed with people. I was nervous about our impending performance. Booda stood quietly and patiently while a little girl tried to uncurl his tail. We watched as our friends each made their runs flawlessly. Then it was our turn. I felt confident; we had practiced and we were in harmony. The run started out great. Booda hit every one of his marks with speed and confidence. He ran through the tunnel, over two jumps, up the A frame and straight under the curtain that separated us from the crowd, and then, right to the concession stand.

My course work at UT had taught me the principles of aqua therapy and introduced me to rehabilitation tools and techniques, but I wasn't completely sure how dogs would handle walking on an underwater treadmill. Booda would help me learn. Booda is so confident and so brave he walked on that underwater treadmill as if he had been doing it his whole life. I would watch him walk and adjust the speed and watch how he would change his gait. I would adjust the water levels making him more or less buoyant. Afterward I would always let him play in the water. From then on, he was all about the water, excluding, of course, puddles, baths, rain or dew on the grass.

Having trained me through my first stage as a practitioner, Booda continued as my test subject for new equipment and therapy ideas. Several years later, the center added a lap pool. The pool was a great addition to our practice. Having a pool would give me a new tool for helping our patients. Warm water releases muscle tension, improves circulation and allows joints to move through the water with no impact. I found myself asking once again how dogs are going to respond to this new therapy.

Pugs aren't known for their great swimming abilities but I had to try it with him. I gathered all of the necessary pool accessories; life vest, goggles, toys, and food. He was definitely curious and was up for new adventures. I put the life vest on him so he would not sink to the bottom of the pool and I tried to put his swim goggles on, but he was having no part of that. I went in the pool with him and placed him on the little step where he could stand without getting all the way into the pool. He would tentatively reach out his paw to test the water and even though there was nothing solid under his feet he jumped in. Not a moment too soon, because Booda would find himself in need of rehabilitative therapy once again.

Booda loved to run around the house like a race track. Circling and circling the coffee table and ending with a leap onto the couch. One day while making his daily turn around the racetrack he jumped onto the couch and got his leg stuck between the sofa cushions. He didn't panic but I could see that he needed help and when I pulled him out he screamed. Afterward, he was limping around the house. An emergency trip to the vet had revealed that Booda had luxated his knee cap.

The knee cap sits within a groove of the thigh bone. Sometimes, in small breed dogs the groove is too shallow and the knee cap will slide in and out of the groove. In Booda's case, due to the malformation and the trauma, his knee cap was permanently displaced and would need surgical repair to put it back in. Again, we found ourselves camped out at the clinic.

Following his surgery, I was much more confident about my skill in rehabilitating dogs. Booda was also conditioned to all of the rehab equipment. As I was preparing for my certification, I decided to use Booda as one of my case studies. Once again, rehabilitation shortened his recovery time. Part of my exam was to present a case to my classmates and instructors. I had seven minutes to present my case to a group of veterinarians and human physical therapists, and I was nervous. Once I loaded my disc and Booda's face came up on the screen, my confidence was restored. Seeing his face gave me courage to stand and present. I think it also softened up my classmates and teachers. Booda's charm and spirit came through again. This time, Booda had helped me to pass my canine rehabilitation practitioners exam. However, this was not to be "a happy ever after story."

Booda's eye troubles started with vague symptoms. He just wasn't himself. He had what I could only describe as a strange look on his face. His ears were always up and his head was cocked as if he was listening intently, trying to understand what you were saying. He would make several trips outside to the deck and quietly sit there by himself. I knew in my heart that something was very wrong, but pinpointing it was difficult.

Strange things started to develop. For example, he did not want to jump into the car, and instead waited for one of us to pick him up. He was also reluctant to go on long walks. At first, I thought these developments might be related to his orthopedic issues. Booda did have an extensive medical history: besides the two orthopedic procedures he needed in his earlier years, the exit from his stomach to his intestines was very narrow so it took a long time for his stomach to empty and sometimes would get acid reflux to add to his discomfort. Then there were the two fainting episodes, which led to the discovery of a heart condition that makes his heart rate slow. We brought him to the vet several times, and nothing was found. I'm sure they thought I was crazy. Our vet did every type of blood work we could think of. We did ultrasound of every abdominal organ and took a chest x-ray to find the source of his troubles.n Everything came back normal. But I still felt he wasn't right.

It wasn't until we moved into our new house that it became very obvious to us that Booda was having significant visual problems. Booda was raised from a puppy in our old house and now, in new surroundings, he was bumping into things like the couch and the coffee table. He was hesitant in dim lighting and seemed confused. He had anxiety about being left alone in the new house. He had difficulty finding us in the new house, even if we were close by. Through these observations, it became obvious to us then that he was having difficulty seeing. But we had no idea the extent of his vision loss and would be shocked to later find out that he was completely blind in the right eye.

When we spoke with our veterinarian she suggested that we make an appointment to see the ophthalmologist. It was apparent to the ophthalmologist immediately that Booda was partially blind. He had no blink reflex in his right eye. A dog's blink reflex is an involuntary blinking of the eyelid in response to a foreign object. Also, his pupil did not constrict or dilate when exposed to light, another symptom of blindness.

It was determined that Booda had good vision in the left eye and this was probably why he was able to compensate so well. The question in our minds was, "Why did he go blind?" Without further diagnostics it would difficult to know for certain. A tentative diagnosis of granulomatous meningoencephalitis (GME) was made. Granulomatous meningoencephalitis is an inflammatory disease that affects the central nervous system. Clinical symptoms can vary depending on which part of the nervous system is affected. Blindness can be a symptom of GME. The cause is unknown. Unfortunately, pugs are in a high-risk category for encephalitis. Because Booda might have a disease involving his brain it was important for us to get an opinion from a veterinarian who specialized in neurology.

We found a wonderful neurologist. She was so kind to Booda and understood our deep bond with our dog. She spent a long time examining him, never skipping the formalities of cookie giving to make him more comfortable. After examining him, she agreed that Booda might have GME, but that the best way to confirm that would be with magnetic resonance image, otherwise known as an MRI. Using a powerful magnet and radio waves, a computer converts the signals into detailed images. This diagnostic tool is great for looking at structure of soft tissue such as the brain. If Booda had encephalitis, the MRI should detect it. Another test that could be done was to get a sample of the fluid surrounding

Booda's brain and the spinal cord and check for the inflammatory cells characteristic of encephalitis. In order to do that, a small needle needed to be inserted very near to his spinal cord to extract the fluid.

We were devastated by the suspicion expressed by two experts, and frightened about what it might mean for Booda's future and quality of life. We decided to proceed with the MRI and prepare ourselves for the worst.

Thankfully, Booda's MRI was normal. There were no areas of inflammation detected within the brain. We anxiously waited for the results of the spinal tap. I had already prepared myself for the diagnosis of GME and was relieved when it came back normal. The diagnosis we were left with was idiopathic optic neuritis. For an undetermined reason, Booda had inflammation or swelling of the optic nerve, a crucial structure in the eye that delivers the message about what the eye sees to the brain. It can happen to any dog and no one knows why. We were fortunate that it had only occurred in one eye.

Booda was put on steroids to help bring down the swelling of the optic nerve and, trooper that he is, he began to adjust to his blindness and to feel much more like himself. He was back to going on walks, swimming and demanding attention. It didn't last long. Three months later Booda developed an eye ulcer. We thought that he might have bumped into something which caused a small hole in the eye and had now developed into an ulcer. Booda was put on several types of eye drops, oral antibiotics and pain medication. A non-healing corneal ulcer occurs when the cells on the surface of the cornea fail to adhere to the underlying tissue. A procedure called a debridement can help to promote healing by removing the non-healing cells. Booda had to have debridement twice. He was not responding to treatment. We were putting medication in his eye every two hours throughout the day and night. The ulcer continued to get worse. One day when I was applying his medication his eye ruptured. The ulcer was too deep and penetrated all the way through.

I tried not to panic, but I knew what had just happened and I knew that he would most likely lose that eye. I packed him into the car and rushed him to the ophthalmologist. Already shaken, we learned the bad news that Booda would have to have his eye removed.

We made our way back to our vet's office and a surgeon was awaiting our arrival. They took Booda into the surgical area. It had all happened so quickly that I didn't really have time to grasp the enormity of the situation. Now, sitting in the waiting room, it hit me. My dog was going to lose his eye. I was devastated. It was all too much. I was overwhelmed with emotion and I broke down. I started crying; I handed my dog to our surgeon and left the building. I had no control issues this time. No internal struggle. I just needed Booda to be well again.

I worried that Booda would also be devastated, that he would be angry, and that he wouldn't understand why we removed his eye. I projected a lot of human emotion onto my dog. Even now as I am writing, I am surprised at my emotion around Booda's enuclation. The truth is that my dog felt better in 48 hours than he had in the last two weeks before surgery. He was comfortable and happy. He wasn't worried about his appearance, or about who would love him or getting a date for the prom. He was pain free and Booda lived in the moment.

Within a few weeks our dog was back to his old self. His sutures were removed and he resumed doing what he loved to do, swimming, going for walks and playing. After his fur grew back, it was even difficult to tell that he was missing an eye. He had already been blind in that eye so he was already adjusted to not seeing on that side. I am amazed at how well he compensated he rarely bumped into things and he was still very bold and confident. Our lives with Booda had gone back to normal. He was regaining his zest for life.

Sadly, it wouldn't last. Booda was having difficulty finding his food and water dish. He was once again hesitant in dim lighting. He began to root around for his food and was having trouble finding us in the house. Within two months of losing his right eye Booda returned to the eye doctor unable to see out of his left eye. This was a huge blow to me and my husband as we struggled to help him adjust, be independent and still be a dog. Initially he was frightened and depressed. Mentally and physically he was no longer the same. This was a very active dog and now he was having trouble finding his food and water dish. He was frightened to go for walks and he didn't like and change to his routine. He wanted to be where I was all the time and was experiencing separation anxiety. He was not interested in playing. He was confused about day and night and he slept a lot.

I felt tremendous guilt. For one thing, I have been a veterinary technician for over 20 years and I couldn't understand why I had not seen the signs of his vision loss. I was sad that my dog would now live in darkness and would never be able to do the things he once loved. Even worse, he would never see me again. I was scared that maybe; somehow, I might love him less. Would other people love him? What could I have done differently? Maybe if he had another owner he would not be blind or maybe I should have fed him a better diet. Maybe I failed him in some way. I was overwhelmed with the responsibility of keeping him safe. I wanted to put him in a plastic bubble. I obsessed about my dog's vision loss for months.

The only encouraging thing for me was to talk to other people with blind dogs. The support of someone who has been through it is very helpful, and their inspiring stories of their own dogs made me feel that I was not alone on this journey. I no longer feel that this is my dog's great tragedy, but an experience I can now share.

So, it was time for me to put my baggage aside to help my dog. I will do my best to try to explain what I believe was my dogs experience as he went blind and our plan to help him live a normal life. I believe that Booda's experiences were similar to mine some sadness, frustration, depression, and anxiety. It is difficult to tell if he was experiencing these things or if he was picking up on the way I was feeling. He has always been a sensitive dog very capable of picking up on our emotions. As he was going blind he wanted to be with me more and he was frightened of things that were out of his routine. After he lost his vision he seemed to be confused about day and night and he slept a lot. He also had a few accidents in the house, which he had never done before. He would also carry his head low looking at the floor, which I believed to be a statement of depression but later found out that it was his way of compensating for his blindness.

We had to develop a plan for Booda that would allow him to trust Tom and me to be his eyes, to trust that we were in control and that he would always be safe. My experience in canine rehabilitation would play a crucial role in Booda regaining his quality of life. It had occurred to me that I could use rehab to help Booda regain his confidence. We had accepted the fact that Booda was not going to regain his sight but how could we help him get the exercise he needed, be mentally stimulated, gain confidence and enjoy life? What was it about rehab that could help Booda?

I thought I would put my training to use. In therapy not only do we assess a dog's physical condition, we also assess their mental status as well. Some of the things I do with patients are to help stimulate them mentally as well. Some of our patients are frightened, frustrated or depressed, and we use some easy, fun games to encourage them. We use games that dogs can be successful at no matter what their physical condition. This is actually a large part of our therapy plan. When my patients are feeling better mentally, they are engaged with their therapy and are so happy to have done something successfully.

I was inspired by a particular patient of mine who began treatment at the age of 17 years. The owner had described her as having "brain fog." This previously active dog had now become inactive and lethargic. She was unable to do some of the things she used to do and was losing her vision. This dog was a thinker, a dog that enjoyed new things and new challenges. I very much enjoyed the challenge of working with her and learned many things from her. One of the things she taught me was that I could use a routine of controlled exercises and brain games to enhance her quality of life, stimulating her mentally and physically. I could see her confidence grow with each accomplishment. Her owner reported that she was once again engaged with life. I worked with this dog until she was 20 years old and I would now use a similar plan to help my dog.

I started to stimulate Booda mentally with some of the techniques we used in therapy. I would wrap squeaky toys in towels and have him try to find them. I would hide food under cups or in paper towel rolls and have him try to dig them out. I would put paper towel rolls on their ends so he could knock them over to get the food or find which hand the food was in. I would put toys in the water and he would wade around trying to find them. I could see his confidence growing. Once we started to see him respond mentally, I began working on the physical aspects. Since he had his confidence back, I thought maybe he could start swimming.

This was a huge exercise in trust for Booda and me. He was completely blind and yet he trusted me. I put a life vest on him and I went in with him. Immediately he knew where he was and was excited. I grabbed a squeaky toy and squeaked it so he could locate me. I shouted "Booda Come" and he did! I immediately grabbed a hold of the handle on the life vest so I could guide him around the pool. He was so happy and free in the pool. We made several laps and then back to the side to rest. He jumped in several more times using the sound of squeaky toys to guide him around. He was thrilled. I was also happy my dog was bold and confident and brave.

I was thrilled that I had found something that Booda enjoyed and a regular routine of swimming helped him to sleep better at night and he seemed less confused about day and night. Swimming was something that Booda had always loved and I wondered if a blind dog could use the underwater treadmill. There was only one way to find out. Again, he was bold and confident I used food to help track him in a straight line on the treadmill. He was incredible. I also started putting him on the therapy ball standing him to increase his core strength and then putting him over the ball to stretch him. I began incorporating some agility equipment into his routine. I have to admit he was really, really brave which was so encouraging to me. Booda was regaining his zest for life. I couldn't have been happier. Although Booda would never regain his vision he now had the confidence to regain his love of life. Booda would have many more adventures and experiences over his life none of them affected by his blindness. We never looked back.

Two years after writing this book Booda passed away at the age of fourteen unrelated to his eye disease. He lived a full and happy life and the lessons I learned from him are invaluable. Sometimes, you get that once in a lifetime dog, the one who teaches you something so profound it changes your life. A little over a year later we adopted Digger a six-year-old blind pug. A wide-eyed, shy, chubby little pug. Much more serious and reserved than Booda but given all we had learned we knew we good give him a good life.

What I am learning from Digger is that he is an individual, a different spirit. I need to find new and interesting ways to engage with him, build and nurture a trust relationship. I look forward to this new journey and I am open to all he has to teach me.

Chapter 1

What Does It Mean to Have Vision?

It's important for me to start by defining what it means to be blind. As owners of a dog without vision, we must have a strong understanding of what our dog has lost. This will allow us to identify the unique challenges that have come up for our dog. For instance, it may be confusing to us that our once interactive dog is now grumpy towards their house mates or a dog who was once confident climbing stairs will no longer do so with the same inhibition. Being blind or visually impaired has its challenges and limitations, but once we identify the new obstacles, we can help our dogs overcome them.

Vision is the ability to see. The eyes themselves are not solely responsible for the full sensory experience that is vision, but rather are tools through which the brain sees the world.   As I discuss how dogs see the world, there are many factors to consider; perception of light and color, visual acuity, depth perception, the ability to detect motion and visual field of view. It is also important to remember that humans and dogs see the world differently. It is possible that canine sight is superior in some areas of visual perception.

How Do Dogs Perceive Light?

The retina, located in the back of the eye, is lined with photoreceptors. Photoreceptors are nerve cells that respond to light stimulus. The retina has two types of photoreceptors, rods and cones. The canine perception of light differs however, because dogs have more rods than cones and humans have more cones than rods. Since rod photoreceptors function better in dim lighting, dogs have an advantage in adapting to low levels of light. On the other hand, cones assist with color perception and are better in brighter lighting making humans function better in bright lighting.

Dogs are also able to see well in the dark because of a structure called the tapetum. The tapetum is located behind the retina and is a layer of reflective cells that acts like a mirror reflecting light back through the retina. Light concentrated back through the retina intensifies vision in dim lighting. Many vertebrates have tapetum, especially animals that hunt at night, who benefit from the enhanced night vision. If you have ever seen the shimmering glow of your dog's eye in a photo or at night, the reflection of light is coming from the tapetum.

How Do Dogs Perceive Color?

Although it was once believed that dogs could not see color, it is now understood that dogs can see some color. Humans see light as wavelengths and we see theses waves as colors. Humans have trichromatic vision which allows us to see a full spectrum of color. The human retina picks up different wavelengths of light which are then translated by the brain into visual color. Humans see light across the full wavelength spectrum, where all wavelengths of light get translated by our occipital lobes into visual color. Dogs have dichromatic vision, which means they only have the ability to see two light wavelengths on the visual spectrum.

A study published by the American Veterinary Medical Association found that dogs do have color sensitive cones, making it anatomically possible for dogs to see some color. Researchers found that these color sensitive cones are able to detect shades of blues and yellows. Dogs cans also distinguish between different shades of grays, but are not able to detect shades of reds, orange or green.

What Is a Dog's Visual Acuity?

Visual acuity is the ability to focus on an object and to be able to distinguish it clearly from another object. This ability depends upon the structure of the eye and its ability to reflect that image clearly onto the retina. Humans have a structure responsible for visual acuity called the fovea located in the center of the retina. On the other hand, dogs do not have fovea.

Recent studies show that different canine breeds have different eye structure. The size and shape of the borzoi eye is different from that of the pug eye. Their retinas differ too. Dogs that have long noses such as the borzoi have visual streak which are nerve cells that run along the width of the retina. Visual streak allows the dog to have a wide field of view as well as good peripheral vision. Having visual streak allows the dog to see movement over a wider landscape, improving hunting abilities. Moving objects come into the dog's peripheral field of view and the dog is able to follow, zero in and chase this desired object. However, having visual streak may make the dog a superior hunter, but it also limits the dog's ability to see in great detail.

Short nose dogs such as pugs have an area in the retina called the area centralis which is a patch of nerve cells that are three times denser than those of the visual streak. Short nose dogs see objects more clearly, but have a smaller field of vision. You are more likely to find your pug watching images on the television than chasing rabbits. This is because they can see the television images more clearly than dogs with visual streak.

What Is a Dog's Depth Perception?

Depth perception is the ability to see three dimensionally, with a clear view of the distance between objects. The ability to have depth perception is dependent on binocular vision. Binocular vision is the field of view where the vision of each eye overlaps, thus creating a single visual image. Depth perception in dogs varies, depending upon the size and shape of the skull. Again, the depth perception of the borzoi will differ from the pug. Dogs with a wide set of eyes will have less overlap and therefore have decreased depth perception. The borzoi may have greater peripheral vision, but less overlap or binocular vision. The pug, with their eyes set in front of their face, may not have good peripheral vision but instead have better binocular vision. Depth perception is important for such things as; jumping, catching, and leaping. Dogs have the best depth perception when looking straight ahead but they may be blocked by their nose at certain angles.

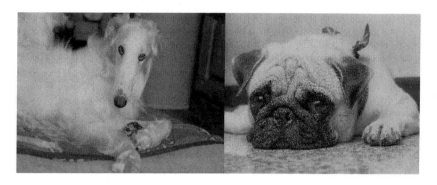

Wide set of eyes   *Eyes in the front of face*

What Is a Dog's Field of Vision?

Like depth perception, a dog's field of vision varies between different breeds due to the difference in the skull shape and the set of the eyes in the skull. For instance, the visual field of a borzoi will differ from that of a pug. The position of the eyes within the skull will also determine a dog's peripheral vision. The pug's eyes which are set more on the front of the face, make for better overlap and therefore better binocular vision. The borzoi, with eyes on the side of the head, has a wider visual field.

Can Dogs Detect Motion?

Dogs can detect form, such as other animals or humans, as well as motion. As previously discussed, some dogs have visual streak which allows them to have good peripheral vision and a wide field of view. Although your dog may not see an object clearly at a distance, they will be able to detect motion. Dogs with area centralis can also detect motion. Although their field of view may be smaller they may see an object with more clarity. Dogs are prey animals, so having good motion detection is a necessary hunting skill. Dogs today do not need to rely much on hunting for survival, but still need to pay close attention to movements of other dogs and their owners. Subtle movements of the hand and shoulder can be used to communicate to the dog. Changes in another dog's body posture helps a dog determine whether this new acquaintance is friendly and approachable or not.

What Does It Mean to Have Low Vision?

A dog with low vision may experience difficulty in one or more situations. Some low-vision dogs see better in lit areas; some are better able to see shadows. Some dogs may see better straight on and others fare better when viewing and object peripherally. Also, some dogs may have vision in one eye and not the other.

Low-vision dogs are not blind dogs, since it implies that the dog has some vision. It may be difficult to know exactly what a low vision dog sees but with proper diagnostic testing and astute owner observation, we can get a sense of what situations are difficult for low vision dogs and provide assistance when necessary.

What Does It Mean to Be Blind?

The definition of total blindness is a lack of vision in both eyes. A blind dog has no ability to perceive light or form such as, structure or shape. Blind dogs have no blink reflex. Blink reflex is an involuntary blink response to stimulus of the cornea. The cornea is the clear part of the front of the eye and its function is to transmit light onto the retina. A blind dog will not be able to blink in response to an incoming foreign object. For instance, if your dog is playing with another dog they could get scratched in the eye accidentally because they cannot blink in response to an object coming at their eye.

The pupillary reflex controls the size of the pupil, and is stimulated depending upon the amount of light entering the eye. A dog that is blind may not have pupillary reflex since they have no response to incoming light and therefore the pupil will not change. Having pupillary reflex does not necessarily indicate vision. For instance, dogs with cataracts may have pupillary reflex and yet not be visual.

A blind dog has no depth perception. Depth perception allows us to perceive objects in relation to ourselves, and helps us navigate the physical world. Without it, tasks like climbing stairs, jumping onto the couch, and other everyday activities are much more challenging. A blind dog also has no visually acuity, no perception of color, form or motion and has no field of view. These limitations can make daily task such as, finding the food and water bowl, the door to outside, and social interactions with animals or people much more challenging. Trauma, as well as many diseases including glaucoma, optic neuritis or sudden acquired retinal degeneration syndrome can cause or lead to blindness.

Chapter 2

Signs of Vision Problems

Signs of vision problems include:

- Discoloration in the eye. A dog's eye should look bright and clear. In addition, the area around the eyeball (the sclera) should be white and the pupils should be equal in their size.
- Excessive squinting or being unwilling to open their eye. Squinting is often the most obvious symptom of eye pain. Pawing at the eye or rubbing their face can also be an indication of pain in the eye.
- Bumping into household furniture. Especially if you have not moved anything around. Dogs that gradually lose their vision are very adept at moving around the home and may not bump into anything because they remember the layout of the home. Sometimes, bumping into furniture does not happen until you move furniture around.
- Hesitation when climbing the stairs, or jumping in the car or onto furniture.
- Hesitation in dim lighting.
- Inability to find the food or water dishes.
- Confusion about whether it is day or night.
- Being tentative in situations where your dog has historically shown confidence.
- Being easily startled.

- Getting lost in the house or in the yard.
- Behavior changes such as; restlessness, anxiety, shaking, shivering or aggressive behavior towards housemates.

If your dog is experiencing any of these symptoms make an appointment to see your veterinarian. Rule out any other medical conditions that may cause these symptoms. Once it has been determined that they are having vision problems it is in our pet's best interest to be referred to the veterinary ophthalmologists. Ophthalmologist have diagnostic tools that are not typically available to our primary care veterinarians. Having a diagnosis is important because there may be treatment available for your dog's condition.

What to Expect at the Eye Doctor

An eye exam may include some of the following tests. Not all dogs will require all of these tests. This is just a comprehensive list of tools available to the ophthalmologist to help them diagnosis eye problems.   Let's take a look at some of the testing available to the ophthalmologist.

A full ophthalmic exam starts with a visual inspection of the eye. Does the eye look clear? Is there any redness or discharge? Is the dog squinting?

Direct ophthalmoscope. A Direct ophthalmoscope is a hand-held instrument that allows the doctor to visualize and evaluate the structures of the eye and magnify the eye up to fifteen times.

Direct ophthalmoscope in use

Indirect ophthalmoscope. The indirect ophthalmoscope uses a hand-held lens and incorporates a small light usually attached to a headband worn by the ophthalmologist. It gives a wider view of the eye and will allow for better examination of the structures in the posterior or inner portion of the eye.

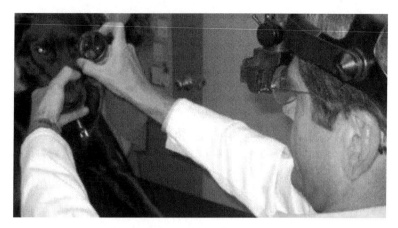

Indirect ophthalmoscope

Pupillary light reflex test. A pupillary reflex test measures your dog's pupil reflex responses to light. Just as in humans, the pupil controls the amount of light that enters the eye. When there is less light, the pupils reflexively dilate or become larger so as to allow more light to reach the retina. When a bright light is shined in the eye, the pupil will reflexively constrict and become smaller. Blind dogs may have an absence of pupillary reflex and will remain dilated regardless of light intensity.

Slit lamp biomicroscope. Slit lamp biomicroscope is a microscope combined with a slit lamp light source. The slit lamp is an instrument that provides a high intensity light. The lamp can be focused to shine light into the eye and the biomicroscope will magnify the structure of the eye and allow you to see the anterior and posterior of the eye.

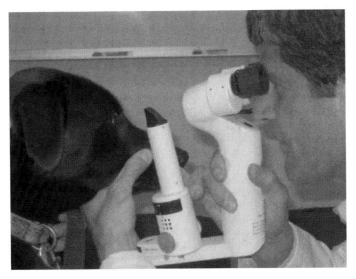
Slit lamp biomicroscope

Schirmer tear test. Schirmer tear test is a test used to determine if your dog's eye is able to produce enough tears to keep it moist. Tear production is important to keep the eye lubricated. This test is usually tolerated well by animals. No local anesthetic is applied in this test as it could give a false reading of moisture production. A small strip of filter paper is placed below the eyelid and is left for about a minute. The filtered paper absorbs the tears and the distance to which the tears flow up the paper is measured tear production.

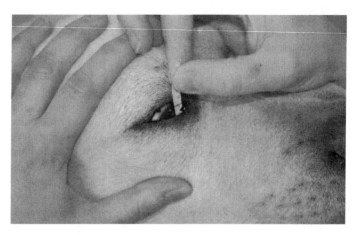

Schirmer tear test

Navigation of obstacles with lights on and off. This is a simple test done to determine how your dog navigates in dim lighting and how he or she will navigate in lit areas. Some dogs follow light shadows and are able to compensate well in an area that is well lit but will be hesitant and unable to find their way in the dark.

Visual tracking. A simple test done to determine your dog's ability to track an object. The doctor may start by having your dog follow an object moving out of their line of vision. Doctors will often use a cotton ball and drop it in front of the dog to see if they can follow it's decent.

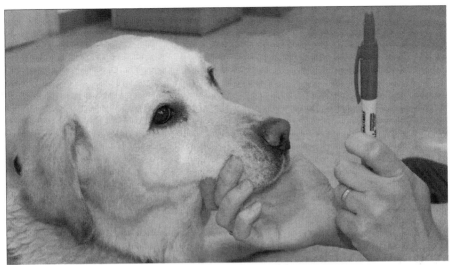

Visual tracking

Fluorescein stain test. This test uses a florescent dye (fluorescein) to determine if there is an abrasion, scratch or ulceration on the surface of the cornea. A slim paper impregnated with fluorescein is slid under the eyelid. When it mixes with the dog's tears it releases the fluorescent dye over the surface of the eye. Next, the eye is rinsed with a saline solution washing away most of the dye. The dye will adhere to any area where the cornea is injured thereby showing the location and size of scratches, ulcerations, or abrasions. While the test itself is not painful, some dogs may resist because their eye is already painful. For those dogs, a local anesthetic is applied first (in the form of eye drop). The anesthetic will then numb the eye making the test more acceptable to the patient. You may notice dye drizzling from your dog's nose a few minutes after fluorescein stain testing. That is because there is a tear duct that drains tears from a dog's eye to its nose.

Tonometry. Tonometry is a simple and pain-free test used to measure a dog's intraocular pressure (pressure inside the eye). It is used to test for glaucoma. A tonometer is a small pen like instrument used to test the pressure of the eye. If the eye is soft, the tonometer will make a small indent in the cornea and the measurement will be normal. If there is excessive pressure within the eye the tonometer will make little or no dent and the measurement will be high. High pressure is an indication of glaucoma. High intraocular pressure can damage the optic nerve leading to blindness.

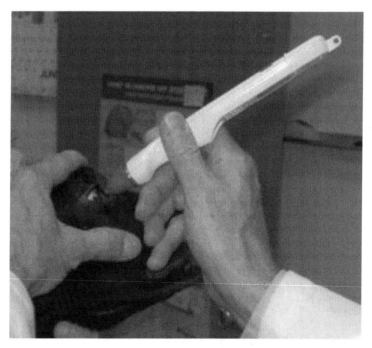

Tonometer

It is also possible that your ophthalmologist may want to do blood work and/or check your dog's blood pressures. Some dogs go blind secondary to a disease such as diabetes mellitus or hepatic encephalopathy. Blood pressures are done to check for hypertension. Blood work and blood pressure will help rule out systemic diseases that may cause blindness.

An electroretinography, or ERG, is a test done to detect abnormal function of the retina. Small electrodes similar to contact lenses are gently placed on the cornea. The electrodes detect electrical activity of the retinas response to light. The retina captures light rays and converts those rays into electrical impulses. An ERG is a useful diagnostic tool when evaluating retinal disorders either acquired or hereditary.

Cytology of the cells of the eye. Cytology is a diagnostic tool in which a sample of cells is collected and looked at under a microscope. A small sterile swab is used to collect the cells from the eye. Examining cells allows the doctor to look for signs of inflammation, infection or cancer.

Magnetic resonance imaging: MRI is a diagnostic tool that will allow the doctor to see structures of the body in greater detail and it is especially helpful when looking at the brain.

Ease the Stress of Examination

If your dog is blind or has low vision, it is helpful to get your dog used to the process of having their head and face handled utilizing the principles of positive reinforcement. This way, eye exams are not a challenge when visiting the vet. You can practice this at home by handling your dog's muzzle, holding their head, looking at their eye and pulling down their eyelid. Make it a positive experience using praise and rewards for allowing the handling. Creating a positive association between two events, such as pulling on your dog's eyelid and then getting a treat, is an example of classical conditioning.

The most famous example of classical conditioning is seen with Pavlov's dogs. While studying the digestive system of dogs, Pavlov a Russian physiologist, discovered that they began to salivate in the presence of food. Pavlov began ringing a bell while simultaneously feeding dogs in order to determining if external stimuli would have an effect on this involuntary response. After extensive study, he found that dogs would salivate at the sound of the bell, even in the absence of food. The dogs associated the bell with being fed, and their digestive system responded as such. When a dog learns that one action leads to another action they make an association between these two events.

It is also possible to change your dog's emotional response to head and face handling as well. In other words, the dog associates handling of the eyelid with cookies. However, handling of the eyelid must predict the cookie. The handling always comes first, followed by reward. If your dog has an aversion to this type of handling this means your dog may have already made an association between two events. For example, your dog may have already made a connection between handling of the eyelid and the pain of getting poked in the eye. If this is the case, you will need to take a few steps back in your training and try to desensitize your dog to this type of handling. In order to do so, you will need to move in slow positive steps and be patient. First, lift your hand in front of the eye and then present the reward. You may need to repeat this step multiple times before being successful. Make sure that your hand is at a distance with which your dog is comfortable. Watch for signs of stress such as; backing away, or flattening of the ears. Remember it is important to progress slowly so that your dog has time to process sensory information. The next step would be for your dog to allow you to place your one hand on their head and eventually progress to having them hold their head still while you gently pull down their eyelid. The time frame for each stage will vary from dog to dog. This does not have to be a stressful event.

There are many things we can do as owners to ensure that our dog will have a positive experience at the vet. Dogs that have had a positive experience at the vet will not be as fearful as dogs that have had a negative experience. Friendly visits have proven to be very affective in minimizing stress for dogs that are frightened. This means the dog goes to the vet's office, comes in, walks around, gets cookies, gets petted by staff members, and then leaves. No shots, no rectal thermometers, no drama, just gaining trust and learning that something bad doesn't always happen at the vet. This makes for a trusting relationship between the dog and staff which is important for future interaction especially if your dog becomes sick.

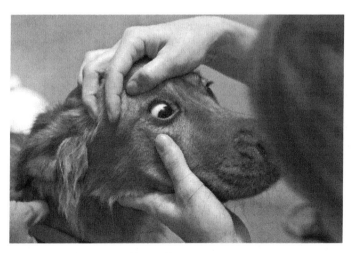

Handling for eye exam

Handling for eye exam

It is a good idea to arrange the friendly visits in advance so that the staff can accommodate you, and the visit can be held when the office is not crowded with other clients.

Also, be sure to address travel anxiety and motion sickness with your veterinarian prior to your appointment. Sometimes anxiety starts with the car ride because the dog is frightened or knows it will get sick.

Be sure to bring the high value treats; a snack something your dog loves but doesn't always get.

We can also teach our dogs to offer a voluntary chin rest. I will discuss more about training in another chapter, but this exercise can help to decrease the stress of examination because this type handling is normal event for the dog.

Voluntary chin rest

Finally, check your emotions at the door. Your dog is an emotional barometer. Dogs are always looking for cues from their humans about what is going to happen next. Blind dogs can detect these cues as well as sighted dogs. If they feel your tension, they may believe that there is something to be tense about. Bringing our own personal positivity into any situation is something that is fully within our control, and it can help our dog also feel a bit more at ease.

Chapter 3

Keeping Your Dog Safe

It is imperative to protect a blind dog from injuries. Dogs without eyesight are more vulnerable to bumping into things and are at high risk for corneal trauma. Blind dogs can also injure themselves, or worse, trip on things, fall down stairs, off balconies, or into swimming pools. It will be your responsibility to provide and maintain a safe environment for your dog.

In the House

To make any home eye-safe, the first thing to do is inspect the home for potential hazards. To do this, get down on the floor at your dog's level and crawl around to see what could be a potential danger to them. This will help you to view the world from their perspective, and give you information regarding their exposure to potential injuries. Here are some suggestions to make a home safer:

- Block off access to stairs, open balconies and open patios. A blind dog could very easily fall down a set of stairs, or have an incident on a balcony or patio. To avoid any of these situations utilize baby gates where necessary.
- Tie up electrical cords so your dog will not get entangled in them.

- Block access to low hanging plants as well as the seasonal Christmas tree (if you have one). Low branches, especially thorny ones, are an eye hazard.
- Do not leave boxes, bags, and other items on the floor where your blind dog might trip on them or bump into them.
- Carry items such as boxes, grocery bags, tools, and gardening equipment high above your dog to prevent eye injury.
- If your dog is low vision, install night-lights throughout the house.
- Do not leave shoes, clothes, toys, or other obstacles on the floor.
- Block off the fireplace area, as well as space heaters and radiators with fire gates or ex-pens.
- Do not leave doors open where a blind dog might wander into an unsafe area.
- Stabilize wobbly table legs.
- Coffee table, end table corners, and the edges of the walls may be easily padded to avoid any injury. Use foam from the fabric store or foam padding that you can buy in the plumbing section of the local hardware store.

Large foam fireplace guard

- If you have a cat that likes to play with your dog, you may want to consider purchasing soft claw nail covers. This will lessen the chances of injury to your dog's eye during play.
- You may also want to put bells on the collars of other pets to alert the blind dog of their presence since a blind dog may startle easily if approached without warning.
- Have a system in place to help your dog find you in the house. In each room of our house there is a different noisemaker for example, if I hear my dog

walking around and I want to let him know where I am, I use the noisemaker to do so. The sound lets him know where I am. If this doesn't work I can also communicate with him via vibration, which I create by tapping the floor.

- Low-vision dogs may be able to distinguish contrast or color. Mark stairwells, stairs and corners with high contrast tape. Place mats with contrasting colors under the dog's bowls and at the top of stairways.
- Keep numbers of 24-hour emergency veterinary hospitals posted where everyone can see them.

It is also important to communicate your expectations clearly to family members and visitors in your household. Inform people who enter your home that your family pet is blind and instruct them on all the safety rules. These should be posted where everyone can see them. Once you have safety measures and a locating system in place, try to keep the furniture layout of the house as it is, at least initially after your dog loses their vision.

While experiencing the everyday joy of living with our late pug Booda, we were able to observe a lot of his habitual behavior. Our dog seemed to have a mental map of the house. He also seemed to have reference points in the house such as the location of the couch, his food dish and his kennel. He did not like to be picked up and moved since he would not know where he would eventually be placed. This caused Booda stress and confusion and increased the chances he would have a mishap and injure himself. We found it important to let him find his way as much as possible. When we did pick him up to carry him, we made sure to return him to one of his reference points.

We can increase our dog's ability to form a mental map with the use of scent marking. Dogs have an extraordinary memory for scent. They have the amazing ability to tell the direction and location of the source of the odor. Marking important spots in the house such as the door to outside, water and food bowls, and crates will help increase your dog's relation to reference points. Scented oils can be used to mark these points. In our home, I used odors that are not offensive to me such as vanilla and lavender. Remember your dog's scene of smell is much greater than yours. You don't need to use very much, and scents may need to be reapplied every one or two weeks. Use different scents to mark different places. Dogs will quickly learn the association between these items and the scent. Scent marking is going to give your dog the best chance at olfactory navigation. When using scented markers, keep in mind that air flow within the home can be a significant factor in the way a dog picks up and tracks scent. It would be ideal to place these scented reference points where there is minimal or no airflow.

The animal-focused medical technology website Innovetpet.com developed pre-scented location markers called Tracerz™ that are convenient, easy to use and safe for dogs. They are self-adhesive and can last longer by being reactivated via scratching the surface.

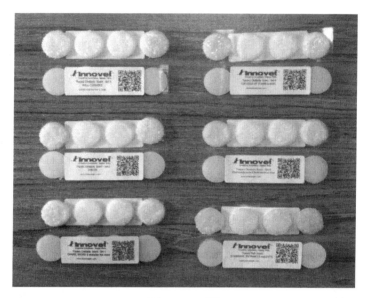

Tracerz ™

To help solidify reference points you can walk your dog around the house on leash. For instance, walk from the bedroom to the food bowl and from the dining room to the food bowl. If you need to rearrange furniture, don't worry, as dogs can learn to remap their environment. Scent marking also helps develop new reference points.

There are also assistive aids available for blind dogs. We were fortunate to find Booda the Littlest Angel Vest©. The vest incorporates a small plastic hoop attached at the shoulders forming a semi-circle around the front of his face. When the hoop bumps into an object, the sensation is transferred to the dog's shoulders and this alerts them that an object is close by. The plastic hoop acts as a protective guard against oncoming surfaces, and gives the dog a way to detect objects before they directly collided into. I like to think of it as whisker extensions, used to heighten perception and allow a dog to feel their way around their environment. In return, the vest can dramatically improve a dog's confidence and also help to minimize nasty head bumps.

Littlest Angel Vest©

Unfortunately, the Littlest Angel Vest is no longer available but there are some great alternatives out currently on the market. Keep in mind that although the vest will help to minimize head bumps, it cannot protect against corneal trauma. To avoid any injury, be sure to follow the safety rules for inside and outside the house.

Digger with Halo for Paws ®

Halo for Paws is a comfortable light wieght vest. It is worn much like a harness and secured with velcro straps and clips at the top. The halo is made of aluminum and is covered with a light weight tubing.

Digger with Muffin's Halo™

Muffin's Halo is another option for halos for dogs. It is also a very light weight easy design. The halo sits on the back of the dog to protect the head and shoulder area.

A great feature of both these product is that the halos have some flexability, providing a nice buffer when your dog bumps into something so that they do not come to an abrupt halt, which could inflict injury. It also makes for less reverberaton to the shoulder making it more comforatble and tolerable to the dog.

Neither design hinders or restricts movement of the limbs or body. Also, be sure to visit their websites to find out how to accurately measure your dog for these aids.

We should also consider that some dogs may not like this type of sensory feedback or sensation. There may be a variety of reasons that may cause a dog to reject wearing a halo vest. This may not be for every dog. However, if that does happen we can help desensitize the dog by using the principles of conditioning. Every time the vest goes on the dog is rewarded creating an association between two events. Wearing the vest equals cookies. Also, try having the dog wear the vest for a short period of time and gradually extend the time. Having this equipment is not only about preventing head bumps but instilling confidence, alleviating fear, maximizing safety, and increasing independence. This is just another tool in your dog's bag and if used properly it can be an aid. Do not leave your dog unsupervised while wearing hoops or halos.

If you are creative and feel you can make a homemade halo here are a few tips. Be sure the design is not restricting movement. Shoulders should be able to have full extension and flexion and should not be hindered. The hoop should be pliable and have some give so the animal does not come to an abrupt stop. Sudden abrupt stopping especially at a fast speed can cause injury. Also, be sure to leave room for your dog's nose. The dog's nose should have some room between the nose and hoop so when the hoop bends it does not hit them in the nose.

Homemade Halo

Crate training was one of the most useful things we had done for our dog, even before he became blind. He had been conditioned as a puppy to think of his crate or kennel as a safety and comfort zone. I also wanted to provide a spot that was just for him. It is safe and comfortable and no one will bother him there. It has proven very valuable in protecting our dog from injury when we are away from home or when something is happening to disrupt his environment such as doing house repairs. We also do not allow our dog to roam around the house at night while we are sleeping. A crate can be put anywhere your dog is comfortable. For small dogs, a soft sided ex-pen can also provide a safe, comfortable area with room to move around.

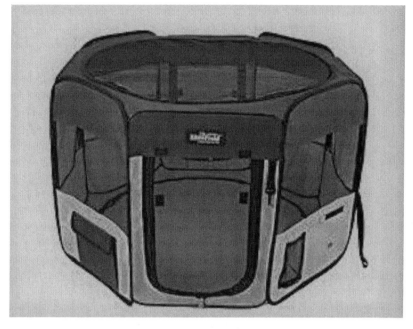

EliteField™

In the Yard

The yard is a different kind of environment with its own list of potential hazards to account for these limitations, do the same thing outside as you did inside. Get down to your dog's level to find potential dangers.

- First, this is important to remember-A fenced yard keeps your dog safe. If that is not possible, consider fencing off a smaller area in your yard where the terrain is evenly distributed. Outdoor playpens or runs are available commercially.

- Steps and uneven terrain can be hazardous to blind dogs. When possible remove tree stumps and also consider leveling and grating your yard.
- If you have a pool or pond, make sure you supervise your dog closely around these areas. Otherwise close it off with a gate so they do not have access to that area.
- Cover all hot tubs.
- Eliminate low tree branches and bushes. Seemingly harmless piles of leaves may have sticks or small branches in them that could cause damage, so these should always be removed.
- Never leave your dog outside alone, either loose or tied up. Always supervise outdoor activity.
- For low-vision dogs an LED light can be added to their collar to illuminate the way, or floodlights with motion detectors can be installed.
- Eye protection: There are several options on the market for eye protection.

Doggles® are safety goggles for dogs. All blind dogs are at risk for eye injury. However, breeds with short muzzles such as pugs, Pekingese and Boston terriers are at greater risk because their eyes are large and bulgy and may stick out beyond their nose. Remember, a blind dog's ability to blink in response to a foreign object is absent. Doggles® will help to prevent corneal abrasion and trauma while also protecting the eye against harmful UV rays. The traditional Doggle® may fit snug for dogs with face pain, eye pain or high intraocular pressure. For those dogs the more flexible breathable mesh Doggle® may be more comfortable.

Doggles®

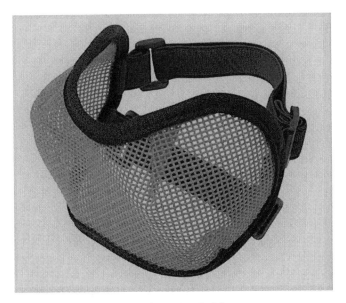

Mesh Dogglel®

I was recently introduced to a product called Rex Specs. Initially this eye wear was made for protecting the working dog, since this breed class can usually be found hiking or hunting but there are several applications for this product. It is protective against blunt trauma, where the large lens guards the eyes and part of the face. The soft foam edge contours to the dog's face, shielding the eye region from dust and debris, and the lens is also protective against harmful UV rays. Since this product is made for the working dog, it is designed to stay securely on the dog during a wide variety of activities, so it is also a great option for active blind dogs.

Rex Specs

Another option for face and eye protection is the Optivisor. The Optivisor is a face and eye shield that helps prevent eye and facial injury. It is used to guard a blind dog's eyes, either just after eye surgery or while they are navigating their environment as part of their daily routine. The Optivisor is also made for short nose breeds such as pugs. If you have questions regarding which eye protection is best for your pet, speak with your veterinarian or veterinary ophthalmologist.

Optivisor™

In the Car

Keeping your pet safe while riding in the car is important. Some dogs ride free in the car but it is safer for all pets to be restrained. There are many seatbelts, harnesses, car seats and crates that can be purchased for safe travelling.

Dog secured with seatbelt

Getting into the car may also pose as a problem. Our dog is no longer able to jump into the car. Luckily, because he is small, we are able to pick him up. If you have a large dog, you may need to guide them or cue them to get in the car with the "go up" command. (This will be described in more detail in a later chapter)

A large dog may also do well with a ramp leading into the car. There are several types of ramps available. A ramp that has good traction with raised sides (to prevent your dog from falling off) will be the safest choice. You may need to practice with your dog, since some dogs are hesitant to use a ramp. The ramp should be stable without movement. An unsteady surface may be scary for a blind dog. Stabilizing your dog's walking surface will alleviate stress for your dog, as a blind dog may view the movement of the ramp as unsteady ground. Use clicker training as a positive reinforcement training tool to help your dog learn how to use the ramp. (See *Developing New Commands*)

In the Neighborhood

When walking our dog, I am constantly scanning the area ahead of us. I want to watch for potential threats; loose dogs, branches, sewer grates, strollers, and even people. Not only do I look for things that might be dangerous, but I also want to get the heads up on any new situation that he may be exposed to. I identify my dog as a blind dog in public. It allows people to recognize him as a disabled dog. Most people will ask before approaching him, so this is a good time to teach people how to greet a blind dog. According to veterinarian Sophia Yin, people should always follow these rules. Stand at a safe distance to appear non-threatening. Approach the dog slowly and ask if you can interact with the dog. Never pet a dog without the owner's permission and also be sure to let the dog make first contact at their own rate.

I teach people that if they want to pet my dog first, they need to let him know they are there with a thigh slap. My dog has come to understand that the thigh slap is a solicitation for greeting.

Then, I let my dog make first contact by approaching or sniffing the new person. Since my dog cannot see, he also cannot interpret human facial expressions or body language. This means he may be unsure of intentions, or may become easily startled, overwhelmed or frightened. If he has made the decision to not greet a newcomer or to get behind me, I respect that. I never force a greeting. If he deems you worthy, you will get a greeting. If not, that's also ok and don't be offended. I respect his space and his decision to not greet or avoid being petted. The same thing goes at home; if we have people over and he retreats to his kennel, I respect his actions and allow him the space he is asking for. I want my dog to understand that I am the leader and I will not let people bother him if he is not up for it. Also, do not allow inappropriate greetings such as hugging, kissing, reaching, grabbing or looming over. These things can be frightening for any dog. It's ok to be an advocate for your dog.

HoundGear™

When walking outside, use commands like "go easy" to slow your dog down and also have him walk beside you. Use the "go up" or "go down" command when approaching curbs and develop a cue that will alert your dog when other dogs are approaching. (See Developing New Commands)

You want your dog to be able to walk with you and not ahead of you. For safety's sake it is best if your dog walks with you. When walking in the neighborhood, I would suggest using an Easy Walk Harness® or Wonder Walker™. Both are designed to gently discourage your dog from pulling against the leash to harshly. Be sure to follow the instructions for proper use and fitting.

Avoid potholes, sticks, branches, and large puddles. Be cautious of sewer grates. Leaves, sticks and debris can cover the opening of a sewer grate and your dog's leg could easily fall through an opening.

Although unlikely, make sure your dog wears some kind of identification in case they get lost. Using a micro-chip or dog tag will provide contact information so your dog may be returned to you.

With Other Dogs

Dogs communicate their intentions not only with vocalization but also with body language. This includes the positioning of their ears, posturing of the tail, raising their hackles, bearing their teeth or wagging their tail and although blind dogs can hear vocal cues, such as; growling, barking, yipping, or yawning they will not be able to see and interpret body language or facial expressions of other dogs they come into contact with. Therefore, they may react inappropriately according to the social conventions of dogs. I have often had clients tell me that they think their blind dog gets picked on by other dogs. With a broad-based stance for balance, forward facing ears positioned to hear what he cannot see, and a lack of eye aversion (in the presence of new company) it is possible that a blind dog may be perceived as challenging to another dog. This is speculation on my part, and there may be many contributing factors as to why a blind dog may be singled out. To be your dog's eyes, you will need to familiarize yourself with basic dog body language. Below I have listed a few postures of canine body language that are important to recognize.

Neutral. A dog in a neutral stance should look relaxed. Their tail will be down and relaxed or wagging, and their gaze will be soft with their ears either relaxed or up. The dog's mouth may be open and relaxed or closed with no tension around the muzzle. This dog is basically relaxed and just hanging out.

Neutral

Play bow. A play bow is an announcement of play. A dog in a play bow will have his or her rear end elevated and their front half lowered, as if ready to pounce. The tail will be up and probably wagging, and the face and eyes will be-soft and relaxed (possibly exposing the tongue). Dogs use play bows before and during a play session. They are essentially stating, "Don't take what I do next seriously, it's just a game."

Play bow large dog

Alert. This is a stance dogs take when something interesting has entered their environment. The ears will be up, the eyes large and staring straight ahead, the front legs stiff and the tail positioned in an upward direction. A dog may also hold their muzzle tight, or have a short tight lip. This is a stance taken by a curious dog.

Alert

Alert with short tight muzzle.

Fear. A fearful dog may have his tail tucked between his legs, his eyes wide open, exposing the white part of the eye, and his ears pinned down on top of his head. A dog that is fearful will make himself appear smaller and will be low to the ground. This dog could potentially bite out of fear.

Fear

Submission. A dog in a submissive position will often roll over on their back, exposing their abdomen. Their eyes will be diverted with their head turned for an indirect gaze. This act of submission is called passive submission. An actively submissive dog will be standing, but will also divert or partially close their eyes, with their ears diverted softly to the side. Their tail will be hung low and they may hold up one of their front paws. An actively submissive dog may also lick or nudge the muzzle of another dog. This is a message to another dog that they do not want trouble.

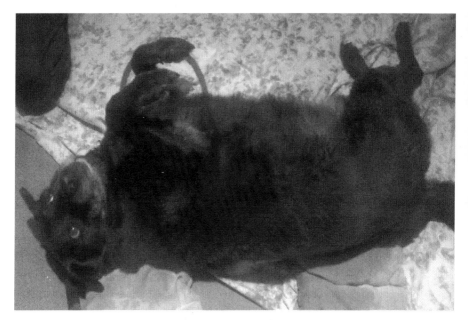

Passive submission

Agonistic Pucker. An agonistic pucker is a warning snarl. A dog with an agonistic pucker will have their lip rolled and teeth shown. It is given as a warning message to other dogs, telling them to "back up and give me space". This warning should be taken seriously by the owner of the blind dogs, as this is a clear signal for increasing distance between the two dogs. If this warning is not taken seriously, it could escalate to aggression.

Agonistic pucker/warning snarl

Aggression. An aggressive dog will have the hair on their back raised, and will be making direct eye contact, rolling their lips and bearing their teeth. The tail will be held stiff and the ears will be stiff and held forward. An aggressive dog will try to appear larger and will be moving forward. If this dog's warning is not taken seriously, this dog will probably bite.

Aggression

Also, be sure to keep an eye out for dogs that have high arousal and low impulse control. These dogs are pushy and often ignore body language or facial expressions of other dogs. They are often barking and pulling at the leash because they are so stimulated.

It's also possible that it could be our dog that has high arousal/low impulse control. In any case, to avoid an altercation I redirect my dog with a treat and start moving in the other direction, giving the "let's go" command.

High arousal/low impulse control

It is also important to remember that not everyone is fully aware of their own dog's body language, facial expression, behavior, or their own behavior. This lack of awareness is dangerous for everyone. In this image, we have a woman out for a jog with her Great Dane on a flexi lead leash about 6 feet in front of her. Body language tells us that something interesting has entered this dog's field of view. The owner may even be yelling "its ok my dog is friendly" to everyone she passes. That might be true, but we simply cannot know for sure. What we do know is that she has no control over this situation or what could happen next.

Great Dane on flexi-lead

Chapter 4
Creating a Comfortable Environment for Your Dog

Limit Accidents in the House

Our dog had a few accidents in the house after he became blind. His habit was to go to the door when he had to eliminate. After becoming blind, he could no longer find the door. In order to maintain normalcy, we had to become more alert to the signals he gave us when he needed to go out. We also decided to put our dog on a regular schedule for going outside. I believe that most dogs who are house trained find it stressful to navigate the decision of either finding their way outside or relieving themselves inside. If our dog did have an accident, it was because we either failed to recognize his signals for wanting to go out or we were off-schedule in giving him the opportunity to go out. Some dogs have better bladder and bowel control than others, as well as less anxiety about any changes in their routine. In our case, even if we had to get a dog walker, we did our best to keep him on a regular schedule of bathroom breaks and meals.

Some people, especially those with a small dog, have trained their dogs to use pee pads or newspaper. In such cases, inside elimination is a normal activity for the dog and their nose will usually guide them to the correct location. So rather than moving the pee pad or papers around, it is better to keep them in the same place.

Carpet runners can be used as a tactile cue which can be introduced with a trail of treats that leads to the door. This is a fun exercise for dogs that are food motivated. Reinforcement and repetition will help with finding their way to the door.

If your dog is not food motivated, you may want to try scenting a trail to the door. You can use scented oils or Tracerz ® to mark the runners and your dog can essentially track their way to the door. Remember that most of the dog's world is observed through smell, so this is a very effective way to help your dog find their way around. If your dog continues to relieve themselves inside, talk to your veterinarian and rule out any medical issues that may cause frequent accidents.

Do not overfeed your dog. Increased food intake equals increased eliminations. Obesity also lead to other health problems that may be detrimental to your dog's quality of life. Pay attention to your dog's urination to make sure that they are drinking enough water. Dogs that have anxiety can develop compulsive drinking habits, which means they drink excessively out of stress and not out necessity. Any amount greater than 4 cups per 20 pounds each day is considered excessive drinking for a dog.

Anxiety

Blind dogs have the propensity to experience fear or anxiety after they lose their vision. They can develop a fear of loud noises such as thunder or fireworks, and can also suffer from anxiety when separated from their owner. Not every blind dog will experience anxiety, but it is important to recognize the symptoms and address them quickly to help your dog through the adjustment period of losing their vision. Symptoms of sound phobias include trembling, pacing, excessive panting and attempting to hide when presented with the frightening noise.

An anxiety attack may manifest itself in the dog as crying, whining, following the owner from room to room, obsessive licking, panting, pacing, inappropriate eliminations, destructive behaviors (such as; chewing on walls or door frames), shredding blankets and pillows, and in extreme cases, self-mutilation. Dogs who have separation anxiety will experience similar symptoms, but the distress occurs only when the dog does not have access to the owner. It is important to know that although separation anxiety can be frustrating, your dog is not doing this to punish you.

Research shows that certain parts of the brain have a central role in the fear response. The thalamus, sensory cortex, and hippocampus, are involved in receiving, interpreting, and storing incoming sensory data. The amygdala and hypothalamus are involved with determining the possible threat, storing that memory and activating the fight or flight response.

Anxiety is the body's natural response to a perceived danger, real or imagined. The body prepares to deal with the danger by initiating the autonomic fight or flight response. The area of the brain responsible for this action is the hypothalamus. The hypothalamus rushes in chemicals such as cortisol and adrenaline and prepares you or the animal to either fight or run. Physically, your dog may experience an increase in heart rate, respiratory rate and blood pressure. Their emotional response is being reinforced on a physiologic level due to the surge of adrenaline. If you believe your dog may be experiencing anxiety, make an appointment to see your veterinarian to rule out any potential illness that may be the cause of these behaviors. Once it has been determined that your dog is experiencing anxiety, there are several options for helping your dog.

1. Be Aware of Your Own Behavior. Dogs are very sensitive to their owner's emotions. Relax yourself before picking up your dog's leash. The leash is like an extension of your arm and the emotions you project will travel to your dog. Try to be aware of your own emotions and anxieties. Remember to take some deep breaths and keep a positive mind set.

Dogs take verbal and non-verbal cues from their owners. If your dog is experiencing separation anxiety, tune in to your own actions to see why your dog may think that you are about to leave. Be aware of the things that you do that indicate you are leaving. Exit cues include; picking up your keys, putting on your shoes or coat, and picking up your purse or wallet. Even though they cannot see, blind dogs can still detect these cues. Try to identify which of your actions may be communicating to your dog that you are leaving. In doing so, you can begin to discover what triggers the anxiety. To help your dog become less reactive to departure cues, do them (listed above) periodically throughout the day while you are home and not about to leave. This will help dissolve the association between the action and your sequential absence right after this action is performed.

Try not to make a big deal about leaving or re-entering the home. Do not greet your dog effusively or allow your dog to excessively greet you either. Dr. Nicholas Dodman, Director of Animal Behavior Clinic at Tufts Cummings School of Veterinary Medicine, recommends ignoring a dog with separation anxiety twenty minutes prior to leaving as well as twenty minutes upon returning.

2. Products that Relieve Anxiety. There are several products on the market that are used to help manage anxiety, which

include Rescue Remedy®, Pet Calm™ and lavender sprays. Rescue Remedy® is a combination of five flower remedies and is usually given a few drops at a time, either on the pet's tongue or in their drinking water. Chill-Out is an aromatherapy spray for dogs that can be used anywhere they spend quiet time, such as blankets, beds, and kennels. Chill-Out is a combination of chamomile, lavender and sweet marjoram. These scents help to calm a nervous dog and invoked a relaxing response. Some other calming sprays will include pheromones that can have an additional calming effect on dogs. Some come in spray bottles and others are available with a plug-in diffuser.

Composure Pro® from Vetri-Science is a great product that can be used to help reduce stress in dogs. The ingredients in Composure Pro™ help promote a relaxing response without causing drowsiness, changing your dog's personality or effecting energy levels. The colostrum calming complex supports stress reduction and cognitive function, L-Theanine helps the body produce other amino acids to bring specific neurotransmitters back into balance; and B vitamins (thiamine) affect the central nervous system to help calm anxious animals. Composure Pro is only available from your veterinarian.

Composure Pro®

The product D.A.P. Dog Appeasing Pheromones® is another way to ease anxiety. Dog appeasing pheromones are synthetic pheromones that mimic the chemical produced by lactating females. This chemical is picked up by newborns and forms a sense of wellbeing, as well as producing a relaxing response, which alleviates fear and anxiety. This pheromone was first identified by Dr. Patrick Pageat, who believes the chemical apaisine is the reason newborn pigs and goats bond with their dams. In his clinical trials, Dr. Pageat found that D.A.P. reduces destructive behavior and vocalization.

Relaxing music has also been shown to help reduce anxiety.

Joshua Leeds, a composer and sound researcher, has become an authority in the field of psychoacoustics. Psychoacoustics is the subdivision of science which studies the psychological and physiological responses associated with sound (including speech and music). Joshua Leeds is the creator of *Through a Dog's Ears*™, a compilation of music that is appealing and soothing to animals. Studies have shown that shelter dogs who have classical music played for them have decreased anxiety levels than those without access to calming music. There are also several studies on the calming effects of harp music in regards to animals with anxiety in zoos, shelters, and pet animals. (See Chapter 6 Stimulating Other Senses)

Another product that is great for anxiety alleviation is The Anxiety Wrap®. It was first developed by Susan Sharpe and Kimberly Ring, and is based on the body wrapping method used by Linda Tellington Jones. The wrap aids in calming a distressed dog, improving body awareness, and decreasing exaggerated responses to sound. Dogs, as well as humans, have sensory receptors throughout their entire bodies. These receptors are responsible for sending signals to the brain so that the surrounding environment can be accurately perceived. The purpose of these receptors is to send signals to the brain about the environment.

Anxiety Wrap®

Touch is one of the most sensitive sensory inputs. The brain responds to these signals by sending messages back to the body on how to respond to the perceived stimuli. For example, if you were to touch something hot, your brain would tell you to pull your hand away quickly. There is a constant system of feedback from the brain to the body and the body to the brain. There are several influences that impact how easily the sensory receptors send messages such as pain, injury, stress or fear to the brain. The continuous pressure of the Anxiety Wrap® calms the sensory receptors by slowing down their hypersensitive response and normalizing the touch responses. The technique of maintained pressure is used in neuro-rehab with autistic children to modify the body's sensory receptors. We tried this with our dog and we were very impressed with how effective it was in decreasing his anxiety. The anxiety wrap has several applications. Not only can it help lesson fear and anxiety but it can all aid in calming a hyperactive dog, shyness or insecurity.

3. Adjuncts to traditional therapy. Acupuncture is a safe and effective way to help your dog with anxiety. Acupuncture is a branch of traditional Chinese Medicine and it is based on the idea that all living things have a vital energy that circulates throughout the body. When an animal or human is in good health, energy continuously flows through meridians, or energy pathways, throughout the body. Each meridian is associated with a different organ system. Acupuncture can be used to fight pain, boost the immune system, or treat anxiety, and it is an acceptable treatment in veterinary medicine. Your veterinarian may offer this service or may refer you to a licensed acupuncturist.

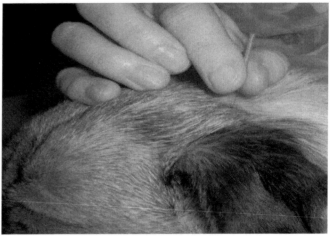

Acupuncture

Another effective treatment for dogs is Reiki, a Japanese healing technique. It is based on the idea that all living things have life force energy that, when decreased or disturbed can lead to illness. The Reiki practitioner will use a "laying on of hands" technique and tap into the universal life energy and channel energy to the patient. This is also something that you can learn to do at home. Reiki is a great human animal bonding experience as well. (See Chapter 6 Stimulating Other Senses)

Another addition to traditional therapy is Tellington Touch® a technique developed by Linda Tellington Jones, a world-renowned animal trainer. T-Touch® is a system that incorporates circular motions over the body along with specific lifts and movements that facilitate body awareness. This specialized system allows dogs to release tension, increase body awareness and reduce responses to fear. I would recommend reading her book, *Getting in Touch with Your Dog*. T-Touch is an effective method for treating fear and anxiety and is widely accepted as a method for improving behavior.

4. Exercise. Another effective tool for fighting anxiety is exercise. Physical exercise is helpful in easing stress. When our dog first became blind he was reluctant to go for long walks and didn't like to walk in unfamiliar places. We began taking him on short frequent walks in familiar places and

gradually extended those walks into new territory. After a productive walk with lots of sniffing, it was always time for a well-earned nap. All dogs, including blind dogs, need exercise. Find things to do that your dog enjoys whether it be walking, swimming, or playing with other dogs.

Also consider physical rehabilitation. Many rehabilitation centers offer helpful modalities (therapy options) that may include underwater treadmill or access to an indoor swimming pool. Modalities, such as the ones previously stated may benefit your dog even if they do not need physical rehabilitation. These activities will allow your dog to exercise in a positive and controlled environment.

5. Anti-Anxiety Medication and Behavior Modification. There are prescription medications available for treating anxiety. This is a subject to discuss with your veterinarian to assure that your dog gets the appropriate medication and dosage. Only a veterinarian can prescribe medications. Be sure to disclose all medications that your dog is taking, including supplements, to your veterinarian before starting new medications. Never give your dog your own medication this is very dangerous and potentially fatal.

Anxiety can be treatable but may require the expertise of a veterinary behaviorist, who will introduce behavior modification and medication. Veterinary behaviorists are trained and certified in the treatment of non-medical related behavioral issues. Behavior modification is based on the idea of changing undesirable behaviors with more desirable appropriate behaviors through reinforcement, sometimes in combination with anxiety-reducing medications. If your dog continues to have anxiety related issues, speak with your veterinarian about setting up a consultation with a veterinary behavior specialist.

When You Need to Be Away from Your Dog

Boarding kennels are not always equipped to deal with the needs of a blind dog. Additionally, if your dog is in unfamiliar surroundings, it will likely create stress. Consider asking your veterinarian for pet sitter recommendations. Veterinary technicians are animal care professionals. Vet techs employed at your local vet's office may be available to care for your pet in your absences. If you need to leave your dog at a kennel, I would suggest making several trips to the kennel with your dog beforehand. This gives your dog the chance to familiarize themselves with the new environment. If a dog is fearful of vet visits, we do this exercise at our practice and have them stop by for friendly visits.

The most important thing is to keep them safe. There is no shame in shopping around to find the most accommodating kennel. Ask for a tour to see where they keep the dogs and also be sure to interview the staff.

Make sure that all staff members are aware of your dog's blind status. Talk to staff about how to support a blind dog and how to keep your dog safe from injury. If you need to kennel your dog bring some items from home that are comforting such as their own bed and their own bowl, as well as something that has your scent on it such as an old t-shirt.

Whatever you end up choosing, be sure to leave a list with emergency numbers, a list of medications or any other special needs your dog may have. You may also want to give your pet sitter or boarding kennel a copy of this book prior to leaving your dog in their care. If you decide to travel with your dog, implement the same safety rules that you use in the home, outside, with other animals and people.

As I mentioned before, products such as Composure Pro® or Rescue Remedy would also be beneficial when you have to be away from your dog or boarding.

Chapter 5

Developing New Commands

If your dog has been trained with hand signals, you will need to develop a new way to communicate with your dog. It is imperative for your dog to learn commands such as: "wait", "leave it", "go down" or "go up". These commands will need to be practiced and you will have to be patient and consistent. Training can be achieved even with an older dog. This is also a great bonding experience for both the dog and owner. It will cultivate confidence, in both the dog and the owner, assuring that you are able to guide and have control of your dog in any situation. Important commands would include words like:

- *Wait*
- *All Clear*
- *Back*
- *Go right or go left*
- *Go up or go down*
- *Leave it*
- *Settle*
- *Go easy*
- *Ready*
- *Come*
- *Let's Go*
- *Go Behind*

How Dogs Learn

Understanding how dogs learn is essential for effective dog training. If you have a good understanding of how dogs learn, you will be able to assist your blind dog in adjusting to new situations.

Dogs learn new commands through repetition and operant conditioning. Learning by operant condition is essentially learning through trial and error. In this type of conditioning dogs learn based on the consequences of their behaviors. Consequences of actions affect future behavior. There are four possible consequences; positive reinforcement, negative reinforcement, positive punishment and negative punishment. It is important to note that when applied to operant conditioning, the terms 'positive' and 'negative' are used as mathematical terms, adding and subtracting. They are not used as terms describing 'good' and 'bad'.

Positive Reinforcement. Positive reinforcement happens when we add a reward after the behavior. The good behavior increases in frequency due to rewarding consequence. The good behavior is strengthened by a positive association with the reward. For example, if your dog sits and then you give him a treat, he is more likely to repeat the sit behavior going forward.

Negative Reinforcement. Negative reinforcement happens when we take something unpleasant away in order to increase good behavior. For example, if your dog is not walking by your side and you jerk the lead, immediately releasing it when the dog complies and walks by your side is considered negative reinforcement. I don't think this method is very effective since it teaches avoidance behavior. Your dog will learn to avoid the leash correction rather than to walk by your side. You are teaching the dog what you don't want him to do, not what you want him to do. This method of training does not promote an effective dog/handler relationship

Positive Punishment. Positive punishment occurs when we introduce something unpleasant in order to decrease a certain behavior. For example, if your dog is chewing on the sofa cushion and you make a sharp unpleasant noise the unpleasant behavior is likely to decrease.

Negative Punishment. Negative punishment occurs when we take something the dog wants and remove it, thus decreasing the bad behavior. For example, if your dog jumps on you to get attention but instead of reciprocating, you turn your back and ignore him, this will decrease the likely hood of repeating this unpleasant behavior in the future.

When training, remember that the reward needs to be something the dog finds valuable, not the owner. Try using a coveted toy or high value treat, something your dog loves but does not normally get.

Clicker Training

The concept of clicker training is to use a two-tone clicker and to click during a desired behavior and then reward your dog for the behavior. This technique is called marking a behavior. Clicker training is a positive training method. Your dog does not need sight to be clicker trained. A very simple description of the formula for clicker training is: get the behavior you want, mark that behavior with a click and then reward that behavior. Once you have marked the desired behavior you can now give it a name or a "cue". For example, if you are teaching your dog to sit, use the "click and reward" whenever your dog sits. Once your dog figures out that they get a reward for sitting they will start offering you the behavior. When the behavior becomes reliable, you can then give it a name such as "sit". Clicker training can be challenging in the beginning. It can be awkward to try and click at just the right moment.

The timing of the click is important. It is essentially letting your dog know exactly what you want. If you are not getting the desired behavior, your timing may be off. Try not to get frustrated since learning takes time and repetition of this method is important for humans as well as canines. Keep practicing. If you feel yourself getting impatient put the clicker down and pick back up later. Keep training session's fun and light for the both of you. If training is fun and rewarding, the behavior will be more likely to increase.

When you are training, start off in a quiet place. Minimize distractions and try not to let people interrupt you during your session. I keep my sessions short, totaling to just a few minutes at a time, so that I can incorporate them into our schedule throughout the day. Make sure to end on a positive note so that the dog finished each session feeling successful.

Make sure everyone in the house is on the same page with training. Let family and friends know not to randomly click the clicker. The sound of the clicker should mean only one thing to your dog - that is your dog being rewarded for something they have done.

If you are having trouble, find a trainer who does clicker training and sign up for a private class. Clicker training is a widely accepted training style and there are a number of books on the market to help you master the technique. If the clicker feels awkward or you are having difficulty marking the behavior you can also use a verbal cue such as "yes" instead of clicking. If you decide to do this, be sure to use the same cue each time. I also recommend reading *Clicking with Your Dog* by Peggy Tillman. This book is very informative, and easy to understand, with step by step instructions on clicker training.

Learning New Commands

Developing a new way to communicate with your dog will be the single most important thing you do to help him adjust to his new blind lifestyle. Also, just because your dog is blind does not mean that is can now be used as an excuse for bad behavior. Your dog still needs to live within the rules of the house. Dogs feel more secure when there are clear rules and defined boundaries. Just because your dog is blind does not mean that they are now incapable of learning new commands.

Please consider the following commands for your dog.

Wait. Training a "wait" behavior with a release cue will improve your dog's safety and also makes the caretaker's job easier. Wait may be used in any circumstance in which your dog needs to stop and wait for your assistance such as; going out the door, at the top of stairs, or while on walks. Your dog should remain in the wait position until you have given them a release cue.

To train the wait command, gently and gradually apply tension to the leash until your dog comes to a stop. Using the principle of operant conditioning, mark the behavior with clicker training followed by a reward for his waiting behavior. Once the behavior becomes reliable, give it a cue, in this case use "wait". Use positive reinforcement such as, "good boy" or "good job". You can also train a release word to let your dog know the task was complete. To train the release word simply give a cheerful "ok" or "all done".

Back. Training the "back" behavior will allow you to have your dog backup on command. Use this command to allow space between your dog and potential hazards such as getting stepped on, falling down the stairs, or other animals.

To teach this command, stand in front of your dog and walk towards them until you gently bump into each other. In response, your dog will take a step backwards. Once again, through the principals of operant condition, get the behavior you want, then mark with a click and reward. Once the behavior is repeatable, give it a formal command name "back".

Right and Left Turn. Training the "go right" and "go left" commands help make navigation on a leash easier. These cues can be used in any situation in where you need to give your dog directional cues such as when the two of you are out for a walk or simply navigating around the house.

I taught my dog to "go left" and "go right" by simply creating a strong association between the words and the corresponding action.   While walking I would tell him left and immediately go left.   It was easier for my dog to learn how to go left than to go right because I naturally walk him on my left side.   During training, I would gently nudge him to the left with my leg.   When turning right, I would often give him auditory feedback by slapping my right thigh and saying "right".   I also made sure to reinforce the left and right directional commands with a game.   To play, I would have him sit for a bit, and then put food to this left and tell him to find it to the left or find it to the right

Go Up and Go Down. Training your dog, the "go up" and "go down" command will increase your dog's safety around stairs. These commands can be used in any situation in which your dog needs to go up or down such as walking up or down stairs, stepping off the curb, or getting in and out of the car. To teach a dog to go up and go down command, use food to guide them to the bottom of the stair where you then place a treat on the edge of the first step. Reaching for the treat may give your dog an idea of the height of the step. First, I would let him get the treat. Then, I would move the treat to the back of the step until it was far enough away so that he would need to step up to get it. For larger dogs you may need to move the treat to the next step, just out of reach, to get them to step up. I wrap everything together, marking the behavior with a click and reward. Once the behavior is reliable, I give it a cue "go up", and praise "good job".

Going down was a little more difficult to train. Remember to be patient when teaching the "go down" command, since it requires a lot of trust on your dog's part and a lot of encouragement from your side. To teach a dog to "go down," reverse the process, putting the food at the back of the descending stair, moving it slowly to the edge until the dog steps down to reach it. I would then mark the behavior with a click and reward eventually giving it the cue, "go down." When training this command do not start with steep stairs. Use stairs that are carpeted and not slippery.   For low- vision dogs, also try marking the edges to the stairs with contrasting tape. This will provide them with extra visual support.

Leave it. "Leave it" is one of the best commands we can teach any dog. This command is especially useful if you accidentally drop something on the floor such as medications or food.

I taught my dog this command by starting off with a piece of food or dog treat that I could pinch with my fingers. When he tried to get the food, I let him sniff it. I would hold onto it and keep it pinched until he would leave it. Once he would leave it, I marked the behavior with a click and reward. When he was able to repeat this behavior, I gave it the cue "leave it," and I would challenge him by moving the food to the floor. When he leaves it, I reinforce it with a "good job"

Settle. The command settle is used when you want your dog to find a place to be calm and quiet. A good time to use this command is when you have company. Start out in a small, quiet room with limited distractions, like the bathroom. Once you shut the door, relax, and ignore your dog. Your dog may seem confused at first, so don't be surprised if they walk around or offer behaviors such as sitting, but eventually they will get bored and lie down. Once your dog settles, click and reward them for this behavior. After you click your dog may get up. Continue to ignore them and once they settle, click and reward again. Once the behavior becomes reliable you can give it a name, such as "settle." Try using this command in increasingly distracting environments. You can also offer a tactile cue such as a hand touch to the top of the shoulder and saying your verbal cue "settle." This will provide your dog with a supplemental affirmation of the command.

Go Easy. Training your dog to "go easy" will allow you to slow them down. Because your dog is blind you want them to stay by your side when out walking. You don't want your dog to walk ahead of you. "Go easy" can be used in any situation in which you need to slow your do down, such as while on walks, when in crowded areas, or while playing with other dogs. "Go easy" differs from the "wait" command in the sense that you do not need your dog to stop immediately, but rather to simply slow down.

To teach the "go easy" command while walking, I would put slow and steady pressure on the leash until the dog slowed down. Once again, I would acknowledge this behavior with positive praise. Using a no pull harness such as the Wonder Walker™ will make it easier to teach your dog to walk with you.

Also, use the tone of your voice to sound like what you are to express as another way to express the expected action of your requests. For instance, the easy command is drawn out as "eeeaaassy" and "leave it" is said more sharply because it is an immediate command and promptness is expected.

Ready. I noticed that when I was about to change commands, I would say the word "ready." For example, if we were walking towards stairs, I would say "ready, go up" or "ready, go down." I began using "ready" to ease my dog from one command to another and it was a routine that developed naturally between us.

Ready is not really a command, but more of a cue that indicates that something is about to change. The reason I list it in this section is because it is what has worked well for me and may be helpful for your dog as well.

All Clear or Free. The "all clear" or "free" command can be used to let a blind dog know that there is nothing in their way. You want to be able to let your dog know when it is okay to roam around freely, without anything in their way. You want to let your dog know when it is okay not to heel and that they are allowed to explore. For this command I recommend going to an open field and use a long leash which allow the dog to roam freely yet still have a connection to you. As you extend the lease say "all clear." This command can be used in the house as well if your dog is tentative about walking around.

Recall or Come. Training your dog to "come" is important for all dogs not just blind dogs. This command can be used in any situation that requires your dog to come back to you. This command could stop your dog from getting hit by a car, getting into an altercation with another dog or any other sort of quickly created potential danger.

To teach the recall command, begin with training simple name recognition. Teaching your dog to recognize their own name will help with recall training. Think of your dog's name as a command, indicating that you would like them to look at you or to orient themselves towards you. Expect visual dogs to make eye contact. A blind dog will not make eye contact, but will ideally turn towards the sound of your voice giving their attention in this way instead. Try using name recognition in increasingly distracting environments. Now that you have your dog's attention you can begin teaching the recall or "come" command.

Begin training inside, preferably in a quiet place with minimal distractions. Teaching recall can be difficult because you need to make yourself more interesting than whatever might have distracted your dog away from you. Have your dog sit or stand in front of you. Back up a few feet and call them to you. For a blind dog you will need to give constant auditory feedback such as slapping your thigh, whistling, or clapping. Try testing some of these sounds to see what is exciting to your dog. This is where clicker training will come in handy, marking the behavior. When your dog repeats the behavior, you can give it a name, in this instance "come" and follow it with praise.

When I train outside, I use a leash just to keep contact with him. In this exercise, the leash is for safety reasons, not for dragging. Resist the urge to pull your dog to you. We want this to be a positive experience and your dog needs to believe that coming back to you is the best thing ever, better than freedom. If the dog has a negative association with coming to you, they will not want to carry through with this behavior. There should never be punishment for your dog returning to you.

Blind dogs can also be taught to hand target. Hand targeting is teaching your dog to touch their nose to your hand. Dogs that are visual will be able to see an outreached hand.   With a blind dog, you will need to have a treat or rub food in your hand for them to have a scent cue.   Use food that has a strong scent like salmon or buffalo. Using the clicker will also help train your dog to hand target. If your dog touches their nose to your hand, click and reward. When the behavior becomes reliable you can give it a name such as "touch."   Say your verbal cue "touch" right before the behavior happens. Once you have taught your dog to hand target, you can use your hand to guide your dog around obstacles, through doorways, or away from danger.

Hand targeting

Once you have mastered hand targeting, you can teach your dog to get behind you with the "go behind" command. Start by having your dog target your hand and then lure them behind you and reward them for being in that position. The "go behind" command can help protect your dog in unpredictable situations. Similarly, if you find yourself in a situation where you need to redirect your dog quickly use the "let's go" command by putting a piece of food pinched in your fingers or closed hand, let your dog smell it, then make a U turn and go in the opposite direction saying "let's go".

Voluntary chin rest. From my perceptive as a veterinary technician teaching the voluntary chin rest is about teaching your dog that hands are not bad and that this type of handing will happen in normal occurrence. Teaching a chin rest can make exams, grooming and medicating much easier.

Start out with one hand straight out and palm facing up. With the other hand lure, the dog with a good smelling treat until they have come right into the palm of your open hand. When the dog's chin makes contact with your hand, use the word "yes" and then administer the reward.

Give rapid fire rewards so the dog learns that they will get paid for leaving their head in position. To get the dog to hold, keep holding the position, taper the rapid-fire reward to a slower rate. The goal is to have your dog leave their head in position for about five seconds and then gradually increase to about ten or fifteen seconds.

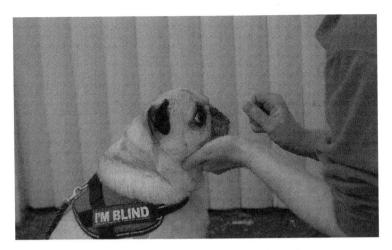

Lure the dog over your hand

Digger with Julius® harness

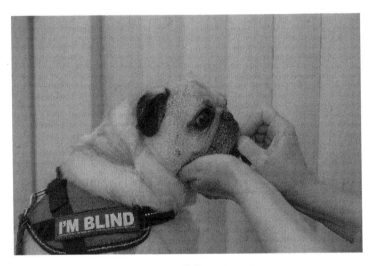

Give rapid fire treats

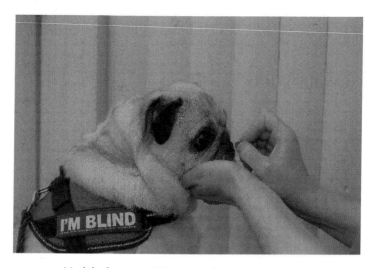

Hold the position and taper reward

How to pair a Touch Cue with a Verbal Cue

Touch cues can be very beneficial to blind dogs. They can be especially helpful in distracting environments or if your dog is experiencing diminished hearing. Verbal cues that your dog is already familiar with can be paired with touch cues. You may have already learned to pair verbal cues with visual cues with a previous dog or prior to your dog losing their vision.

Here is an example of pairing a verbal cue and a visual cue when asking your dog to sit. Give your dog the verbal cue "sit". At the same time you are saying "sit" give a visual cue such as with your arm down by your side, palm facing upward, bend your elbow up as if you are going to touch your shoulder.

Sit with verbal and hand signal

Once your dog sits, mark the sit behavior with a verbal marker "yes" (or if you prefer clicker training, mark your sit behavior with a "click") and immediately follow up with a high value treat, toy, or verbal praise

Marking the behavior you want with a verbal "yes" or a "click" lets your dog know that is the behavior you are looking for. Reinforcing the behavior with high value rewards will motivate your dog. Your dog will come to understand that both the verbal and visual cues mean the same thing.

For blind dogs, the same pairing can be taught with a touch cue, giving your dog a verbal cue and a touch cue at the same time. First you should establish what you want your touch cue to be. I prefer a gentle brush or petting-like motion to my dog's lower back and hips. You can also use a one-finger touch, but remember, any touch cue that you choose must be gentle and not startling or aversive to your dog. Never push or force your dog into the sit position.

Here is an example of pairing a verbal cue and a touch cue when asking your dog to sit. Give your dog the verbal cue "sit". At the same time you are saying "sit" you give a touch cue such as gentle swipe or petting-like motion to your dog's lower back and hip area.

Once your dog sits, mark the sit behavior with a verbal marker "yes" (or if you prefer clicker training, mark your sit with a "click") and immediately follow up with a high value treat, toy, or verbal praise

Just as with pairing visual cues your dog will come to understand that both the verbal and touch cues mean the same thing.

You can use the same formula listed above to pair touch cues with other verbal cues your dog already knows well. For example, you could pair a touch cue to your verbal "down" cue. Again, you will need to choose what you want your "down" touch cue to be. I prefer to use a gentle swipe or petting like motion down my dog's shoulder.

Here is an example of pairing a verbal cue and a touch cue when asking your dog to lie down. Give your dog the verbal cue "down". At the same time, you are saying your verbal cue "down" you give your touch cue. In this case a gentle petting or swipe like motion to your dog's shoulder.

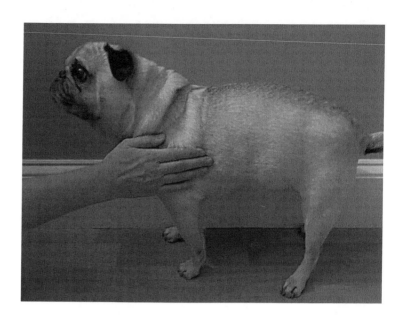

Once your dog lies down, mark the down behavior with a verbal marker "yes" (or if you prefer clicker training, mark your down behavior with a "click") and immediately follow up with a high value treat, toy, or verbal praise

If possible, practice the pairing of cues approximately 3 to 6 times throughout the day. Keep training sessions short, no longer than 5 minutes at a time, and always keep it fun.

You can continue to pair touch cues with all the verbal cues that your dog already knows. Just make sure to choose different touch cues for each behavior so that it is clear to your dog which behavior you are asking them to do.

Remember to go slow, be patient, give your dog time to

figure it out. You will be surprised at how the small successes can go a long way with a dog's confidence.

Training should not be traumatizing for the dog or the owner. If you are having difficulty, consult with a dog trainer, but be sure you are aware of and agree with their training style before starting an actual training session. I highly recommend a positive training style. To find a trainer who uses a force-free method of training, go to www.karenpryoracademy.com Also, check out videos from Miki Saito at www.blinddogtraining.com

Chapter 6
Stimulating Other Senses

Stimulating other senses through environmental enrichment involves manipulating an animal's environment to satisfy physical and physiological needs. Environmental enrichment helps to decrease stress, increase physical activity and stimulate a dog's normal typical behaviors.

Typical techniques used to stimulate environmental enrichment include, food-based enrichment, sensory enrichment, the use of novel objects, social interactions, and positive training. There are many things we can do to enhance our dog environment.

Aromatherapy (Smell)

As I have discussed previously, dogs experience a large part of their world through their enhanced sense of smell. A dog's sense of smell is highly developed and can detect smells that humans cannot. Because of their superior nose, we have been able to train dogs to track, hunt, rescue, sniff out drugs, blood and food. Some dogs are even being trained to sniff out cancer cells.

Dogs sniff to maximize their odor detection, inhaling to trap odor molecules. Dogs take in air through each nostril and they expel that air through the slits in the side of the nose. The ability to smell through each nostril gives the dog the enhanced ability to determine not only what smells are in their environment but also which direction the odor is coming from.

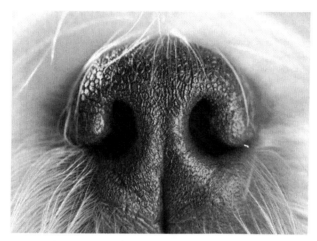

Dog nose

A dog's nose has two nasal cavities. Within these nasal cavities are rolls of cartilage and bony tissue called turbinates. The turbinates are lined with ciliated epithelial cells. The cilia are hair like and help to trap odors and send signals to the brain. Located on the roof of the mouth is a unique "sense of smell" organ. The anatomic term for this unique feature is the Vomeronasal Organ or the Jacobson's Organ. This Vomeronasal Organ aids with detecting pheromones, providing information about the opposite sex. If you have ever seen a dog or cat sniff something and open their mouth, they are utilizing their Vomeronasal Organ.

Why is sniffing so important to dogs? It's how they "see" the world. Sniffing gives dogs information about their environment. It is very natural and pleasing for a dog. Sniffing gives them input about other animals, humans, and plants. All of these things are meaningful to your dog and make them happy.

Sniffing

There are many ways to stimulate your dog's sense of smell. The idea of aromatherapy is relatively new in veterinary medicine. Nevertheless, some recent studies offer evidence that validates aromatherapy. Dr. Deborah Wells conducted a study on dogs with travel induced excitement.

Thirty-two dogs were observed for three consecutive days. During the first condition, the dogs were exposed to no odorant and during the second condition they were all exposed to the ambient odor of lavender. The results showed that when the dogs were exposed to the scent of lavender they spent more time resting and sitting, and less time standing and vocalizing. In 2005, a study was done testing four essential oils lavender, chamomile, rosemary and peppermint. Fifty-five dogs housed in shelters, were exposed to one of these oils each day for five days with two days of no exposures in-between. The dog's behaviors, vocalization, body positions and activity levels were recorded.

The results indicated that dogs seemed more relaxed and barked less when exposed to the scent of lavender and chamomile. The scent of rosemary and peppermint seemed to act as a stimulant with dogs being more active and vocal.

There are many natural ways to stimulate your dog's sense of smell. Allow your dog time outside to air-scent and sniff. These things may not seem pleasant to us, but it is very natural and pleasing to a dog. In an article in the Whole Dog Journal, Randy Kidd, DVM PHD, stated, *"The best nutrition we can give to a dog's nose is a daily dose of natural odorants, generated from field and woodlands. Outdoors is* the perfect way to build up the reserve of sensory cells and brain connection related to smelling."

Music Therapy (Sound)

Studies have shown that the playing of music can influence animal behavior. Dogs are sensitive to external rhythms and their internal organ rhythm will increase or decrease in response to it through a process called entrainment. Entrainment is the synchronization of the body to an external rhythm. The body essentially sets its internal rhythm to the external vibrations or rhythm. Entrainment is the phenomenon that explains how music affects us.

Noises such as sirens, lawnmowers, thunder, fireworks, and motorcycles can overload a dog's sensory input. On the other hand, playing classical or harp music will help to relax a dog. In human studies, classical music was shown to affect pulse and heart rate and to reduce negative emotional states. In a 2002 study to determine the effect of music on dogs, five different types of auditory stimulation were used-human conversation, classical music, pop music, heavy metal music and no music at all. What they discovered was that dogs were more relaxed, barked less, and rested more when listening to classical music. Dogs that spend time listening to heavy metal barked more and spent more time standing.

Dogs that are blind and deaf can also benefit from music therapy through vibration. Although soothing, not every dog reacts the same to music. Observe your dog for relaxing responses such as stretching, and sleeping. Dogs may also become desensitized if music is played constantly.

Experiment with dog toys that make different sounds. Water bottles and plastic milk containers make a fun crinkling sound. Other toys giggle, squeak, or make animal noises. There are even toys that can record your voice. Switch toys around to make it interesting. To make old toys seem new take them out of rotation and reintroduce at a later time. Take note of what sparks your dog's curiosity and supervise play.

Drinking fountains can also be used. The running water drinking fountain will help if your dog is having trouble finding their water bowl. Some dogs enjoy drinking from running water and some dogs need to get used to the idea of drinking from a fountain. If you decide to change your dog's water bowl to a fountain be sure they are using it and getting enough water. The water fountain should be placed where your dog can access it easily, perhaps where the old water dish used to be. If you are concerned about your dog drinking enough water, place other water bowls or fountains around the house along the route of your dog's mental map or reference points.

Sound can be used as cues for dogs. Thigh slapping, floor tapping, or clapping can cue your dog about direction, your location, or the location of other objects such as the food or water bowl. For instance, if your dog is having trouble finding their food dish, tap the bowl with a spoon so they can follow and track the sound. Dogs are tuned into sound all around them. When I open the refrigerator, my dog suddenly appears. Picking up my keys is an exit cue. Floor tapping gives my dog cues about my location. Sound cues are a valuable source for owners (assuming your dog has hearing) and may be more reliable as a cue than scent marking because scents can dissipate and air flow can disperse scent affecting the way dogs pick up and track scent.

Tactile (Touch)

Dogs get information with touching. By using their mouth, whiskers, and tongue, they socially interact with other members of the pack. Whiskers are a dog's sensory organs. Whiskers are sensitive to vibration and air current. The whiskers themselves do not contain nerves but the bases of the whiskers have nerve endings sending information about the dog's environment back to the brain. Dogs can also experience touch with their paws and the rest of their body. Some different ways to stimulate touch are:

Rug runners. Use runners as tactile cues in the house. Rug runners can be used as trails that lead to important things such as the door, the food bowl or water dish.

Massage. Massaging your dog is a wonderful human/animal bonding experience for the both of you. Massage relaxes the body and relieves tight muscles. Massage can help to lessen anxiety, or comfort a frightened animal. Some dogs may not want to be massaged, therefore never force massage on an animal that has refused it.

Textures. Experiment with different textures of toys. There are thousands of dog toys on the market. Plush toys, latex toys, toys made out of old fire hoses for dogs that require durability in their toys. You will find an array of interestingly textured dog toys. By trial and error, you will find ones your dog enjoys most. Mix them up frequently to make it interesting.

Touch cues. Touch cues can be used in combination with verbal commands. They can replace verbal commands in noisy environments or if your dog is experiencing decreased hearing.

Touching your dog is good for you too. Petting a dog or cat helps to lower human stress levels and lowers blood pressure.

Food (Taste)

Dogs do have taste buds. Sometimes it is difficult to believe seeing what some dogs will ingest. When compared to humans, dogs have fewer taste buds, so their sense of taste is not as sensitive as humans. As I mentioned previously, dogs enjoy the process of smelling, therefore, they seem to enjoy things that have good smells. The ability to taste gives your dog information about the palatability of foods. Taste also stimulates the salivary glands and stimulates the gastric system. Some important notes about dogs and food:

Dogs have the ability to detect sweet, sour, salt and bitter. Dogs tend to dislike things that are bitter or sour and prefer tastes that are more savory flavors such as meats. However, there are always exceptions to that rule.

Treats that have strong odors, such as liver or fish, are often appealing to dogs.

Foods that have strong odors can be used to play tracking games with your dog. Treats can be used as a "treat trail" helping your dog navigate your home. Try treats that have a variety of flavors.

Experiment with foods that have different textures. For instance, uncooked green beans are crunchy and bananas are soft and mushy.

Some foods contain antioxidants, fatty acids or vitamins that may help support the structures of the eye. Yellow or orange vegetables such as carrots, sweet potato and squash are rich in Vitamin A. Fish such as mackerel and tuna are rich in Omega 3 fatty acids. There are no conclusive studies to suggest that Vitamin A is beneficial to the health of the canine eye. There is, however, evidence to suggest that it is beneficial to the human eye. Omega 3 fatty acids do show an anti-inflammatory effect.

Keep in mind that most dog foods are already nutritionally balanced and do not require additional supplementation. This is purely an exercise in stimulating taste and not recommendations for diet change.

Be cautious of how you feed your dog. As owners we want very much for our animals to experience joy and happiness and we want to be the ones to provide that joy. Because blind animals are not able to do some of the things they used to, some owners have a tendency to substitute those things with food. It is extremely important that we do not over feed our animals. Animals that are obese are at greater risk for cardiac disease, high blood pressure, diabetes, and gastrointestinal problems. Increased body weight puts additional strain on bones, muscles, joints, tendons, and ligaments and may shorten your pet's lifespan.

Check with your veterinarian before introducing new food or treats to be sure they are appropriate snacks for your dog. There are some foods that can be toxic and dangerous to your dog, such as chocolate, onions, grapes, or raisins.

Putting it all together

To stimulate all of these senses we can create a sensory garden for our dogs. This gives the dog an opportunity to use their natural senses such as smell, hearing, touch and possibly taste. Engaging in these activities is mentally stimulating, fun and interesting. It may also help to ease stress for dogs by engaging in normal typical behaviors such as, sniffing, air scenting, listening, and exploring. The idea is to make an interesting outdoor environment by providing things for your dog to engage in. Such as adding nontoxic plants for sniffing, wooden chimes for a soothing sound, an area for digging, hiding treats in the grass for the dog to find or add a place for sunbathing.

Sensory garden

Do your research to be sure there are no toxic plants in your garden. Implement the safety rules for outside. The ASPCA has a list of plants that are toxic to dogs and cats at www.aspca.org/pet-care/animal-poison-control/toxic-and-non-toxic-plants

Reiki (Energetic)

Reiki pronounced as (ray-kee), is a Japanese healing technique developed by Mikao Usui. Reiki means universal or life force energy. Usui developed a hands-on healing technique that taps into universal energy and can be channelled through the practitioner to a patient. This transferring of energy is believed to aid in the balancing of energy within the body, aiding healing. Usui believed that Reiki could be used to bring healing on a physical, mental and spiritual level in people. Reiki is often used as an adjunct or complement to conventional medicine. Even though its validity is still being studied, it is often offered by hospice, hospitals, doctor's offices and veterinary practices. A study done at Harvard University in Cambridge, Massachusetts showed that people who received Reiki prior to cardiac catheterization reported feeling more confident and relaxed. Doctors also reported that patients were more cooperative. Anyone can learn to do Reiki and it is something that can be done at home. A synopsis:

- Reiki enhances the human animal bond
- Reiki is not harmful
- Reiki can help reduce anxiety.
- Reiki promotes a state of relaxation.
- Reiki can promote an overall state of well being
- Reiki can be used as an adjunct to traditional medical therapies.

Reiki should not be used as a substitute for seeking veterinary attention for your pet.

Making Life Enjoyable

Play

Playing and social interaction are important for dogs. Play is not only fun but it helps dogs to expend pent up energy. It is physically and mentally stimulating and it's a great stress reliver. All dogs need an outlet for energy. Your blind dog may not be able to do some of the things they used to do such as, chase the frisbee, so it's important to find new ways to engage your dog. Let's take a look at some fun and interesting was to play with your dog.

Swimming. Swimming is a great strengthening exercise and it is great fun.
However, safety is paramount. Be sure you are able to reach and control your dog in the water. Life vests can be worn to provide buoyancy. Bring a squeaky toy with you as it provided auditory feedback making it easier for your dog to swim towards you. Do not force your dog to engage in this activity if it frightens them.

Some dogs do not enjoy swimming but rather wading in and out of the water. Dogs may also enjoy water play in a child size swimming pool.

The Buster Food Cube. The Buster Food Cube can be filled with treats or kibble. As the cube rolls around the floor it dispenses food. This is a great game for blind dogs as they can chase it around by following the sound of the cube on the floor and track the food when it comes out.

Hot & Cold. Hot and cold is similar to tracking, but your dog will learn to take cues from you. Start off with letting your dog sniff some food or a coveted toy. Then hide it. Make it easy to find at least in the beginning. As your dog moves closer to the object, tell him he is getting hotter or moving away, getting colder. Hot and cold is similar to tracking but your dog will learn to take cues from you.

Find Me. Have your dog try to find you. Use auditory feedback such as clapping, whistling, or tapping the floor. Use lots of praise for finding you. This is a great game for reinforcing the left and right command. Have your dog sit and then put a treat either to the left or right, then I tell them to "find it right" or "find it left." Again, we are using a game mentality to reinforce training, but also making it fun.

Hide a toy in a towel. The toy should either have a squeaker or have some sort of scent. Wrap the toy up in the towel and have your dog try and get it out. Make it simple to unwrap with lots of praise for finding it. Once your dog has figured out the game you can make it more difficult.

Nose Games. As I have discussed previously, dog's experience the world largely by their sense of smell. Nose games are a way to utilize that great sense of smell in a way that is fun. Put treats in an empty paper towel roll and stuff both ends with paper towels and have your dog try to figure out how to get it, or get some empty toilet paper rolls and stand them on their ends putting treats in some of them and having your dog knock them down to find the ones with treats in them.

The Snuffle Matt. The Snuffle Matt is designed to stimulate a dogs natural foraging behavior, engaging your dog physically and mentally. By sprinkling food or treats throughout the mat the dog engages their olfactory senses while searching for the food. Sniffing and foraging for treats engages your dog in a natural and pleasing way.

Paw5 © Wooly Snuffle Matt

Use toys that stimulate thinking such as Nina Ottosson brain games. There are a variety of toys available in this line that a blind dog can enjoy. Although these toys are not specifically designed for a blind dog, they were designed to mentally stimulate your dog. Just because your dog is blind, does not mean they do not need mental stimulation. Blind dogs get bored too.

Some of the recommended toys include the *Dog Brick, Dog Tornado, Dog Smart, Dog Magic and the Dog Spinny*. The object of most of the brain games is to figure out how to get the treat sometimes by moving blocks, moving flaps or turning discs. Usually these games are taught to dogs by allowing them to see where you have put the treat and then they figure out how to get them. In the case of a blind dog, let them smell the treat and have them bring their nose right down to the level of the toy when you hide the treat. Also, be present and interact with your dog. This should be a fun thing for both of you. These toys are designed for owner and dog interaction, so be sure to supervise your dog when playing these games. Interacting increases the fun and the chances of your dog success. You can also develop this game at home by buying a large muffin tin and put treats in the some of the tins and cover them with tennis balls, empty Kongs® or plastic cups.

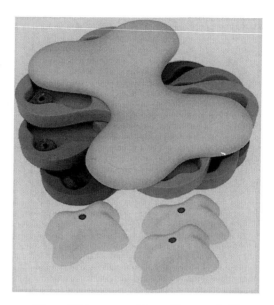

Nina Ottosson Dog Tornado®

Nose work. In canine nose work, dogs learn to search for a specific scent and to locate its source utilizing the dog's ability to track odor and their desire for hunting. When I do nose work with my blind dog it always sparks interest from other dog people. Nose work is a fun and interesting way to stimulate your dog's natural ability to detect and locate the source of odor. Nose work is like hide and seek with your nose. It starts with getting your dog engaged in searching for a food reward hidden in one of several boxes, then expanding the search area. Eventually, your dog will be trained to target odors such as birch, anise, and clove. This is a great way for dogs to gain independence, problem solving skills and confidence. Blind dogs present unique challenges such as stair climbing, leash walking, and the introduction of new people and places. I want my dog to feel confident not only in himself, but in me to be his eyes. He needs to trust that I am the leader and I have established my role as leader in a positive manner through training and nose work.

Being blind, our dogs need to be able to maximize their other senses, and to give them the best chance at doing that we can help him by stimulating those senses. Doing nose work helps dogs build up sensory cells related to smell. Essentially building a data base of smells. This data base of smells helps them navigate. For instance, in the home I use pre-scented location markers. Digger has learned the association between the odor and the item it is attached to. These have become his reference points in the home and give him the best chance at olfactory navigation.

Nose work teaches dogs how to problem solve. Problem solving is an important exercise in mental stimulation and it is just as important as physical exercise. Problem solving is also a huge confidence booster.

There is some evidence to support the thought that dogs are happier about receiving reward after problem solving versus just receiving the reward. Dr. Ragan McGowan for the University of Agricultural Sciences, Sweden, conducted a study with beagles and the results showed that dogs that engaged in problem solving and earned rewards appeared happier, wagged their tails more, and were eager to repeat the exercise as opposed to dogs that were just given rewards.

The researchers noted that, "The experimental animals in our study were excited not only by the expectation of a reward, but also about realizing that they themselves could control their access to the reward. cThese results support the idea that opportunities to solve problems, make decisions, and exercise cognitive skills are important to an animal's emotional experiences and ultimately, its welfare."

Nose work is open to everyone and your dog does not need to be visual to participate. However, safety is a primary concern. Our instructor is very aware, as are my classmates, to what might be hazardous for Digger and they make accommodations for him. If you want to try nose work, speak to an instructor first and audit a class be certain that you agree with their style of training. Nose work training should not be traumatic for the dog or the owner. Ultimately, it's about having fun by stimulating your dog's natural ability to hunt and find the source of odor. Get out there, have fun, and build a better relationship with your dog - blind or sighted.

Play with Other Dogs

Dogs love to play tag, tug of war, and wrestle and chase each other. If you have more than one dog you may have experienced the joy that dogs can get from one another. However, not all dogs will get along.

If you only have one dog and would like to arrange play dates, have your dog's meet in a neutral location. Take them together on a walk in neutral territory rather than at your house or their house. Bringing dogs to a neutral place lessens the likelihood of viewing the new dog as an intruder in their territory.

When introducing new dogs to each other, keep them on leash. Each dog should be controlled by a separate person. Don't do it alone.

Be observant of your dog's and the other dog's body language. As previously discussed, be alert to dog body language. Things can start out friendly and change quickly. You need to be alert to protect your dog.

Be aware of your own body language. If your dog senses that you are tense they might believe that there is something to be tense about.

Introduce your dog to another dog that has proven to be dog friendly. It is a good idea to have dog friends that might be about your dog's size for safety.

Teach your dog a cue that another dog is approaching, such as "puppy" or "doggy" it can be any word you like as long as it is used constantly. If you have a friend with a dog friendly dog, you can practice having that dog approach your dog each time using the same command.

If your dog enjoys playing with other dogs, should you get another dog if you only have the one? Some blind dogs do very well with another dog in the house. I have heard incredible stories of animals assisting another animal. I have no doubt that the animals that are blind or deaf take cues from other animals, essentially acting as a seeing or hearing aid dog. Just because your dog is willing to play with another dog does not necessarily mean they will be accepting of another dog in their home.

If you are thinking about adding another dog to your pack Patricia McConnell Ph.D says consider these things:

What impact will adding another dog to the family have on the resident dog? We need to consider things such as; does your dog like other dogs, what play style does your dog have and will it match with another dog. Does your dog share toys, bowls or attention well?

Think about what type of dog would fit your lifestyle and fit the dynamics of your household. For instance, if you have a mellow, old blind pug, a tenacious rat terrier may not be the best match. What effect will a new do have on your family? Do you have enough time to devote to another dog? Blind dogs may need to be walked separately depending on their confidence, stamina and routine.

Have a backup plan. Do your homework on what to do if things between dogs do not work out. Consider incorporating your trainer in the choosing and introduction of new dogs to your household.

Dog's relationships can be complex and clicker training can help establish your role as the leader in a positive manner. Be careful in your choosing. Think about what type of dog would fit your lifestyle and fit the dynamics of your household. Having another dog can be a fun and rewarding experience for both you and your dog. Blind dogs can take cues and play with other dogs but make sure the match is right for you and your dog.

Rehabilitation

The reason I felt it was important to mention rehabilitation in this book is that it follows my line of thinking about treating the dog as a whole, building confidence, and increasing quality of life. Rehabilitation is both physically and mentally stimulating and allows your dog to exercise in a controlled environment.

Obviously, this is not going to restore your dog's vision, but rehab has a lot of great benefits. We have the ability to relieve tight, painful muscles, and retrain gait. We can increase range of motion, strength and endurance. While you might not associate these symptoms with blindness, think about how you might alter your body while walking in the dark when you can't see where you are going. Blind dogs often over extend their forelimbs when walking so they don't bump into things. Much like you might extend your arms when walking in the dark so you don't bump into things. If your dog alters their gait or become less active, your dog could be experiencing some of these symptoms: tight or painful muscles, muscle atrophy, decreased range of motion, decreased strength and endurance. Clients report that their dogs were not only mentally and physically stimulated but they also were gaining confidence through rehabilitation. Here are some examples of modalities available for your dog.

Massage. Massage is a manipulation of muscle tissue through a series of hand movements such as stroking, gliding, rolling or kneading. Massage will help to relive tight, painful muscles, increase lymphatic flow, and reduce muscle spasms. Massage may relieve anxiety or distress. It is also a good body awareness exercise.

Stretching. Stretching improves range of motion, promotes circulation, improves coordination and prepares the body for movement. Stretching prepares your dog to go from inactivity to dynamic activity. Stretching increases flexibility. I recommend reading *A Healthy Way to Stretch Your Dog* by Sasha Foster and Ashley Foster.

Passive Range of Motion. Passive range of motion is a technique used to maintain or improve the flexion and extension of a joint. Not having full range of motion can limit a dog in their movement.

Underwater treadmill. Walking on the underwater treadmill provides exercise in a controlled environment. Strengthening exercises can be done by walking, using the resistance of the water to gain muscle strength. In turn, the water provides buoyancy allowing an animal to walk but not have to bear full weight on their limbs.

Therapy ball. The use of therapy balls is helpful in stretching and strengthening your dog. Simple exercises that can be done at home will help to maintain muscle mass, strengthen muscles, improve your dog's overall core strength, and increase balance.

ToeGrips. ToeGrips are little rubber cylinders that fit onto a dog's toenails and provide traction on slippery surfaces. ToeGrips provide traction and gripping in a way your dog's toenails cannot and they can be a great aid for dogs with visual or mobility impairments.

When applied, ToeGrips make contact with the floor creating a "GripZone" which is just behind the bottom of the nail tip. When dogs are given the ability to gain traction through their own natural mechanism, gripping the floor with their toenails, the results are renewed confidence.

Illustration provided by ToeGrips.com

Tile and vinyl flooring can be slippery for any dog, but for blind or physically impaired dogs it may limit their ability to move around the home. Rug runners can be strategically placed around the home to help with traction. However, this is not helpful when our dogs are at the vet, groomer or if they lay down on slippery surface and cannot get up. As a veterinary technician, I see dogs skate across the waiting room floor desperately trying to grip with their toenails. This can be a very frightening for any dog and the fear of falling is real. This fear can affect a dog's confidence when navigating the home.

Why should we be concerned about our dog's confidence? According to Dr Julie Buzby the owner and inventor of ToeGrips "It directly correlates with quality of life." Fear, isolation, anxiety and feeling helpless affect a dog's quality of life. Dogs that are limited in their ability to move around the home, interact with family members, or get left behind when other dogs go out for walks can experience some or all of these things. Dr. Buzby feels that dogs become fearful on floors for at least 3 reasons:

History has taught them that gaiting these floors results in falling. The dog has made an association between gaiting the floor and falling. They become conditioned to predict the fall and that's scary. Imagine if you fell every time you stepped out onto your front porch. You would dread going out there. Dr. Buzby states. "There is a constant struggle against the potential that gravity has to take them off their feet. This is 'running in the background' every time they gait on these floors. "

If a dog has slipped on the floor, it may have been painful and they remember that event. Even if the dog slips but doesn't fall there maybe pain associated with that event. If you have ever slipped on ice you know that even without falling it can be a painful event, twisting your ankle or hurting your back. Dogs are quickly conditioned to avoid repeating that painful event.

It is a dog's natural response to flex the paws to create traction. If that reflex fails and dogs are unable to grip, it can be a frightening experience. Imagine falling and not being able to grab onto something to stop that fall and how frightening that can be.

According to Dr. Buzby, dog's that are mobility impaired such as, geriatric dogs, arthritic dogs, or dogs recovering from surgery do not have normal compensatory mechanisms. Young, healthy dogs are able to compensate in other ways that senior or mobility impaired dogs cannot. For instance, a young healthy dog is going to be able to regain their balance were a senior dog or dog recovering from surgery will not. It's a dog's natural response to flex the paw and dig in the nails essentially gaining traction but if that mechanism fails due to diseases such as osteoarthritis, trauma, or neurologic disease they cannot grip.

ToeGrips give dogs the ability to move without fear or apprehension, reducing the possibility of injury, increasing function and being able to engage with things that bring them joy such as, social interaction and play.

There are many techniques utilized in canine rehabilitation. To find a canine rehabilitation practitioner in your area, go to The University of Tennessee's website **www.canineequinerehab.com**.

It is important that you have someone who is trained and qualified to treat your pet. Physical rehabilitation should be done in a controlled environment by a professional rehabilitator. There are situations where these treatments are not appropriate and need the expertise of someone who is trained in this field.

Chapter 7
Ethical Issues for Caretakers Consideration

Commitment

Having a pet takes commitment, but having a pet that is disabled may require a more fervent commitment on your part. Having a disabled pet takes patience and time. It will require you to teach your dog new things, new commands, and how to handle new experiences. It may require you to rearrange your schedule, get up early or stay up late. It will require you to teach and educate your friends and family. Having a blind dog will require creating and maintaining a safe environment.

You will need to continually nurture a trust relationship between the caregiver and the disabled pet. Pets who are disabled may need more medical attention than the average pet which may mean higher medical expenses.

Providing emotional support for your dog is another important aspect of commitment in owning a blind dog. Your pet's confusion or anxiety can be disheartening. Some blind dogs can become depressed. Some blind dogs become very needy. Your dog will be looking to you more than ever for guidance, leadership and support.

There are also your own emotional aspects to deal with:

- A disabled animal can bring you to despair, especially when you see them struggle.
- A disabled dog will change your expectations of having a dog. I admit that, sometimes, I am jealous or sad when I see other people doing things with their dog that I would like to do with mine, but cannot.
- Not everyone will accept your decisions regarding your dog. (There is a misconception that having a blind pet is cruel.)
- Having chosen to keep a blind dog, one feels obligated to make life enjoyable for that dog.
- I miss eye contact with my dog. I miss the bonding experience of looking into each other's eyes.
- It's ok to admit it's hard. It can be. It's okay to ask for help. It makes it easier if everyone in the household is on the same page as far as taking care of and helping your dog. If you feel that you are unable to handle the commitment, ask friends, family or neighbors to help out. Animal people are sympathetic to the needs of animals and you may be able to find a good resource by just asking. There is also a website, **www.handicappedpets.com,** that offers support to owners of handicapped or disabled dogs. There is a whole community of people out there willing to share their experience and offer guidance. A good example

is **www.blinddogs.com**. There are several Facebook groups that are dedicated to blind dogs as well.

How to handle hurtful comments

If you have a blind dog, you may have gotten them. Hurtful comments such as: "oh that poor dog", "You know there are plenty of healthy dogs in the shelter waiting for homes", "You should put him/her down", etc. I can only surmise that people make those comments because they are uneducated about blind dogs and have some misconception that blind dogs aren't happy, or that having them is unfair or cruel to the dog. I obviously disagree, since I have now owned two blind dogs. My dog's blindness has not had a huge impact on his comfort level. I would say his quality of life ranks very high. My dog is blind, otherwise he is just like any other dog. Lack of vision is not a measurement of contentment, nor should it be. Having a sensory impairment does not equal suffering.

So, why respond to these comments? Yes, it is rude however, if we could educate or change even one person's mind about living with a visually impaired dog we could save a dog's life. We need to dispel myth's such as; blind dogs are not adoptable, that they will not have good quality of life, or that they cannot adjust to being blind.

If we could change this person's view about disabled dogs, they may tell someone else about meeting a blind dog and how happy and well-adjusted they were. Take a deep breath, refrain from angry thoughts and educate.

I explain that my dog has been taught how to handle new experiences. He is well adjusted and trusts me to be his eyes. I have established my role as a leader in a positive manner. My dog walks, plays, and swims, he has a bed in every room, he is allowed on every piece of furniture and he also does nose work, which he loves. This is what makes my dog content. We need to stop equating sensory impairments to suffering. Educating people instead of responding in anger might change someone's mind about blind dogs. There are many dogs living full lives with some type of sensory impairment or physical impairments.

1. Although your defenses are up, stay calm. Don't argue with the person, educate them instead. Explain your dog's condition. Sometimes, people are able to relate to diseases such as cataracts or glaucoma. Perhaps, they even know someone with these conditions.

2. Teach them something. For instance, a dog's primary sense is smell and this is how they get information about the world. Hearing is likely their second most relied on sense and they are very heightened to sound

and the direction of sound. These senses help them navigate their environment even when they can't see.

3. Show them something. A trick your dog can do or how your dog walks on a leash. I once had someone stop me because they were impressed my blind dog could go down stairs. Seeing a blind dog do dog things is impressive, so show it off. It also helps solidify what you have been stating all along that blind dogs can live happy well-adjusted lives.

4. If you are simply too angry, walk away and don't engage. You don't have to tolerate rude unsolicited comments. If the opportunity presents itself to educating someone, great, if not, walk away.

More often I am approached with genuine questions, compliments and occasionally, people will thank me for adopting a blind dog. Be open to answering questions. Be proud of your dog's accomplishments. Go out and have some fun with your dog.

Quality of Life

We have the ability in veterinary medicine to end suffering by euthanasia. However, this leaves owners with a major responsibility. When is the right time? Is it right to end an otherwise healthy animal's life? Quality of life is an extremely important issue to pet owners and this has been repeatedly expressed by our clients. How do we assess our animal's quality of life? The quality of our pet's life is not only very personal but also highly subjective.

Even though my dog is blind, I believe his quality of life to be good. I have to admit that I was worried in the beginning about what my dog's quality of life would be. There is an opinion among some people that keeping a blind dog is cruel. I disagree. I believe that he has everything that he wants which is mostly to be with Tom and I. His blindness has not had a huge impact on his comfort level. Having said that, I also don't know what it is like to have a blind dog that is a working dog, sporting dog or a high-performance dog. This kind of dog may be more challenging than my pug and your experience may differ from mine. It is my belief that in the absence of other diseases, blind dogs are not suffering from being blind. However, there are other factors to quality of life.

Dr. Frank McMillan author of *Mental Health and Well Being in Animals* describes quality of life as a balance between pleasant and unpleasant experiences. Like humans, dogs will have many experiences within their lifetime, some good, and some bad. When the scale starts to tip towards mostly unpleasant experiences, we then need to evaluate a dog's quality of life. Unpleasant experiences can include pain, anxiety, fear, isolation, depression, and helplessness. Blind dogs that are limited in activity or new experiences, or who are isolated can experience some or all of these things.

How to Access Quality of Life

This is most certainly a conversation that should be had with your veterinarian.   While blindness itself may not equal suffering, there are many factors to quality of life. There are some diseases that result in blindness that may cause us to contemplate our dog's quality of life. For instance, idiopathic optic neuritis is not a painful disease, but dogs that are blind from uncontrolled diabetes may experience a diminished quality of life.

I will give a few things to think about to start the dialog with your veterinarian. At our practice we are constantly evaluating and re-evaluating quality of life issues. Most of our patients recover, however, some of our patients are geriatric, are paralyzed from neurologic injury or have a terminal illness. We work closely with our veterinarians to help our clients assess the quality of life of their pet.

- Is your dog still engaged with life? Meaning are there still things that your dog enjoys? (Walks, playing with other dogs, food etc...)
- Does your dog have a disease that causes uncontrolled pain?

- Does your dog have a disease for which there is no cure?
- Does your dog outwardly express aggression?
- Do you have reasonable expectations?
-

In rehabilitation, we often discuss expectations with owners. Some people expect that their 15-year-old dog will want to play Frisbee again. Your dog may not want to or be able to do the things they once enjoyed. This does not mean your dog has a poor quality of life. For a blind dog, it may be a matter of finding new things that your dog will enjoy.

We use a very simple quality of life scale, called the HHHHHMM scale. (Taken from *Canine and Feline Geriatric Oncology* adapted from Villalobao, A. E. Quality of life scale)

1. Hurt: Is your dog in pain and if so is the pain adequately controlled? This is without a doubt one of the biggest concerns of our clients. Pain management in veterinary medicine has changed quite a bit over time. We have a wide variety of non-steroidal anti-inflammatory and analgesics drugs. There are also drugs that can be used to enhance the non-steroidal anti-inflammatory medication. Some of the larger veterinary hospitals provide pain management clinics. This raises the question. How do I know if my dog is in pain? Pain is not always easy to recognize. Some dogs are very passive

about pain. Signs of pain might include restlessness, crying, panting, and reluctance to walk. Some dogs may become needier while other dogs might hide. Dogs that are not usually aggressive may become tentative or grumpy. Dogs that have eye pain might squint, rub or paw at their eye.

2. Hunger: Is your pet eating or are they refusing food? Are they receiving the nutrition they need? Some dogs are picky about food, and dogs will often not eat when they are not feeling well or in pain.

3. Hydration: Is your pet drinking enough water to stay hydrated? If your dog is blind, are they able to find the water dish?

4. Hygiene: Are you able to keep your pet clean after elimination? Is your pet grooming? Dogs that are immobile for long periods of time can get pressure sores and this could become a source of infection.

5. Happiness: Does your pet express interest or are they engaged with you or the family? Are there things that bring them joy?

Cookie

This is Cookie. She was our foster dog. Having been badly neglected, she was removed from her home. Cookie had many medical problems and she was mostly blind. She was considered unadoptable and was going to be euthanized when she was adopted by the caring staff at The Sterling Impression Animal Rehab Center - including myself. We were told she would probably only live one year. We wanted to give her the best year we could. She was so happy she lived five more years!

6. Mobility: Can your pet get around or does he need assistance? Decreased mobility alone does not indicate

poor quality of life. I have many patients that are in wheelchairs or have amputations but are still very engaged with life and their quality of life is very good.

Penny

This is Penny. Her owner rescued her knowing that she had a spinal cord injury. Penny began rehabilitation and got an Eddie's Wheelchair. She walked two miles every day and was very happy and well loved. Her mobility impairment did not diminish her quality of life.

7. More Bad Days than Good: When the bad days outweigh the good days, it may be time to consider having the discussion about quality of life with your vet. Keep a journal and make a note every day and review your notes often.

If you believe that your dog may be suffering or in pain, discuss it with your veterinarian. Keep a journal of your dog's good days and bad days. It's hard to remember the good days when you're having a really bad day. Also, remember that when your pet first goes blind, there may be more bad days in the beginning. They need time to adjust and so do you.

Enucleation

Enucleation is a term used to describe the surgical removal of the eye. I am putting this in the book because I know from personal experience how overwhelming this can be to an owner. If your dog is facing enucleation, it is probably because there has been trauma or disease of the eye for which there is no treatment or causes pain.

Owners often face the decision to remove the eye under stressful circumstances, such as trauma. In the case of trauma there is little time to think about the decision to do surgery. Making the choice to remove my dog's eye was very difficult, although I knew it was the right thing to do. As a technician, I knew that his eye was painful and non-functional, essentially useless to my dog. As an owner, it was difficult to think of my dog with a missing eye.

Enucleation

It's important to remember that our dogs don't carry the same baggage we do. Our dogs are not worried about how they look. They aren't worried about getting a date, or a job. My dog's pain was alleviated within 24 hours after removing his eye. There may be a misconception that dogs that have had their eye or eyes removed have a poor quality of life. Eneculeation is not an indication of poor quality of life in fact, just the opposite it will improve your dog's quality of life if they have pain that cannot be controlled due to trauma or disease.

If your dog is facing an enucleation and there is time to do so, it would be worth it to ask your ophthalmologist if you could arrange to meet and talk with other clients whose dogs have been through the procedure. It's encouraging to see other dogs with enucleations doing well and it can be a bit overwhelming to see your dog at first without their eye. After the eye is removed and the sutures are taken out the skin may sink inward so there might be some indenting in the eye socket. Once the incision is healed and fur has grown back, you may not notice it. People didn't even notice that my dog is missing an eye at first. Some conditions that might require enucleation include glaucoma, deep eye ulcer (melting eye ulcer) trauma or proptosis.

There are orbital prosthetics available. This procedure includes the inserting of an orbital prosthetic. This includes a sterile prosthetic ball to be inserted prior to the closing of the eyelids. The prosthetic will prevent the lids from sinking. This procedure should only be performed by an ophthalmologist and is not recommended for every dog. Flat faced dogs with large orbits and shallow eye sockets, such as Pugs, Boston terriers and Pekingese may not be good candidates for prosthetics. It is also not recommended for dogs with infections of the eye socket. Keep in mind that with any prosthetic in animals there is always a possibility of rejection or failure which may result in another surgical procedure to remove the implant.

Dogs that have a disease such as glaucoma may qualify for a procedure where the interior of the eye is removed and replaced with an implant. This implant will leave your dog with a bluish gray colored eye. Talk to your ophthalmologist to discuss and decide the best option for your dog. Keep in mind that having an implant is for aesthetic purposes only. It is not painful for your dog to be missing an eye.

Ultimately, your dog's comfort is most important. To find out if your dog is a candidate for orbital prosthetics, speak with your veterinary ophthalmologist.

Pixie Toy Fox Terrier with bilateral enucleations

Pixie, the Toy Fox Terrier had glaucoma that was not responding to treatment. The pressure in her eyes caused her pain and the owners made the decision to have bilateral enucleations. At the time of surgery, Pixie had orbital implants. One implant failed and the other had to be removed. Pixie never looked back she is pain free and living the good life. She runs in the backyard, can get on the couch and boss her brother around. She did not experience any of the symptoms of anxiety that my dog did. This is a good example of how different dogs deal with vision loss. Being blind does not appear to cause her any distress. She relies on her mental mapping in the house and yard and her sense of smell. Meeting this dog, it is difficult to tell she is blind. She is amazing.

CHAPTER 8

What to Do in an Emergency:

- Don't panic. Stay calm.
- Keep your pet calm.
- Do not allow your dog to rub or paw at their eye.
- If your dog has punctured or scratched their eye seek immediate veterinary care.
- If your dog has dislocated their eye do not try to put it back in.
- Seek immediate veterinary care.
- If your dog's eye has been penetrated by a foreign object, do not try to remove it. Seek immediate veterinary care.
- Do not use any over the counter eye medication without seeking the advice of a veterinarian first.
- Seeking veterinary care could save your dog's vision, do not hesitate to get help when regarding eye injury.

How to administer eye medications

Giving eye medications to any dog can prove to be challenging however, as I discussed previously, it is possible to change our dog's emotional responses to this type of handling.

Practicing the steps, handling of the muzzle and face, and voluntary chin rest I have outlined in *ease the stress of examination*, will assist in assuring a positive outcome.

Once you have mastered handling your dog's face, muzzle and eyelid, your dog should not have an aversion to this type of handling because it has made a positive association with it. Consider the following tips:

Be sure to read the instructions prior to administering eye medication. You do not want to wait until you have your dog in position and ready to go and then have to read the instructions.

Positioning the dog between your legs will allow you to have two free hands.

Place one hand under the chin and lift upward so the eyes are towards the ceiling. Be certain not to let the tip of the medication bottle make contact with the eye.

Squeeze out the prescribed dose and then reward with food, praise or toys.

If you are having difficult try practicing these things, break them down into individual steps. Practice each step one at a time until you can move onto the next step. Be patient, don't be tense, and make it a positive experience.

Chapter 9
The Future for Blind Dogs

The future for blind dogs is looking bright, with new studies and new development on the horizon. In 2016 an assistant professor of ophthalmology at North Carolina State University College of Veterinarian began a two-year study into sudden acquired retinal denegation syndrome.

Dr. Freya Mowat will be investigating the role the immune system and hormones play into the disease. According to Dr. Mowat "Veterinarians have diagnosed sudden acquired retinal degeneration syndrome for more than three decades but we still don't understand it well enough to try to develop effective treatments," This gives great hope for developing better diagnostic criteria and for the treatment of dogs affected with sudden acquired retinal degeneration syndrome.

In 2106 Dr. Sara Thomas at UC Davis California began conducting clinical trials into identifying protein biomarkers and/ or the genetic components of the disease sudden acquired retinal denegation syndrome. If there is a genetic component to SARDS this gives great hope for the future in developing test to identify which dogs carry the gene and breeders will be able to select dogs for breeding who are not carriers of this gene.

There is also advancement in the development of products for blind dogs such as; nutraceuticals, navigation tools and head protection.

Ocu-Glo™. *Ocu-Glo™* is a nutraceutical that was developed by two board certified veterinary ophthalmologists and a compounding pharmacist. Ingredients include grapeseed extract, (does not include toxic grape skin) lutein and omega 3 fatty acids. This product may help to slow the progression or prevent diseases such as sudden acquired retinal degeneration, immune mediated retinopathy, progressive retinal atrophy and uveitis. Who should take *Ocu-Glo™*? Dogs with diminished vision, a cloudy appearance to the eye, cataracts or dogs that are predisposed to eye diseases such as glaucoma. This is not a cure for blind dogs, but it is the first time a balanced nutraceutical has been available to help lessen the ocular damage caused by disease and possibly slow the progression of vision loss.

The Blindsight devise is a 3D imaging transmitter. That works on the principles of echolocation. Echolocation is the use of reflected sound to determine direction and distance between objects. Your dog does need to have hearing for this devise and although I have not tried it yet I think this is a promising tool for blind dogs. **jordycanid.com/origin**

The bumper hat is customized padded headgear for dogs. Acting as protection from nasty head bumps. The Bumper hat is partially helpful for dogs that require padded head protection such as, dogs with neurologic conditions, hydrocephalus, protection from thrashing post anesthesia, seizures or dogs with cerebellar hypoplasia. Check out www. missionpawsable.weebly.com for more information.

The following is a picture of my friend's ducks Petunia and Daisy. Petunia, on the left, is blind from cataracts and Daisy is her seeing eye duck. They are inseparable. Petunia follows Daisy and Daisy is Petunia's guide. My point being that Animals are amazing and their ability to adapt is incredible. Just because your dog is blind doesn't mean they are broken, make time to spend with them, find something you both enjoy and have some fun!

Petunia and Daisy

Chapter 10
Anatomy of the Eye

Having an understanding of the structures of the eye will help you to have a better understanding of your dog's diagnosis. Any interruption to the health or transparency of the structures of the eye could lead to partial or total blindness

The Front of the Eye

The dog eye is very similar to the human eye in its makeup. The eye itself sits within the folds of the eyelids. The eyelids have many purposes, including keeping the eye free from foreign material and housing the tear glands, which keep the eye lubricated. The inner part of the eyelid is called the conjunctiva and it prevents foreign material from getting behind the eyeball.

The outer most part of the eye is called the cornea and the white dense connective tissue that surrounds the eye is the sclera. The cornea serves to protect the eye and focus light. Light rays enter the front of the eye through the cornea. The cornea bends light to focus onto the retina in the back of the eye.

Behind the cornea is clear fluid called the aqueous humor. The aqueous humor inflates the eyeball and nourishes the cornea while maintaining intraocular pressure. This part of the eye is the anterior chamber.

The Middle of the Eye

The iris is the colored part of the eye and is a muscle that shrinks and enlarges the hole in the middle called the pupil. By making the pupil bigger and smaller, the iris controls the amount of light going into the eye it becomes larger in low levels of light to allow more in and shrinks in bright light to keep some out.

Behind the iris is the lens. This part of the eye does just what it sounds like it does; it focuses the light traveling into the eye so that it is a sharp image when it hits the back of the eye. The lens is able to focus by changing its shape. Muscle fibers called the ciliary body are responsible for altering the shape of the lens. The tissue that lines the inside of the middle of the eye is called the choroid.

The choroid is very vascular and supplies blood flow and nutrients to all the structures of the eye. The middle of the eye is filled with a jelly-like substance called the vitreous humor. The vitreous is a clear gelatinous substance and allows light to pass directly from the front part of the eye to the back of the eye. This part of the eye is the posterior chamber.

The Back of the Eye

The back wall of the eye is called the retina and it is like a movie screen, receiving the images coming into the eye through the pupil. The retina consists of cell receptors called rods and cones. They collect light and transform the light into nerve impulses.

It is interesting to note that the image passing through the lens is focused on the retina upside down and the brain actually puts it right side up. In fact, vision is not a function of the eye; rather the eye is the tool through which the brain "sees" the world. The final part of the eye is the optic nerve. This is the pathway that an image projected onto the retina follows to the brain itself.

Appendix

The Eyelid: The eye or the globe sits within the folds of the eyelids. The eyelid consists of the upper, lower and third eyelid. The eyelids house the lacrimal glands. The lacrimal glands produce tears and keep the cornea from drying out. Within the eyelid there are also ducts that allow for the drainage of tears. The third eyelid is a protective membrane and is located under the eyelid. It adds protection for the eye by its ability to close upward and cover the eyeball, keeping the eye free of foreign bodies. The medical term for the third eyelid is the Nictitating membrane. The third eyelid is visible when the eye retracts into the eye socket. Examples of diseases of the eyelid include:

- Entropion
- Keratoconjunctivitis
- Nictitans Gland Prolapse
- Eptopic Cilia

Entropion is an abnormal inversion of the eyelid. It can occur in one or both eyes. It most often affects the lower eyelid; however, it can occur in the upper lid. Symptoms of an entropion include rubbing, excessive tearing, squinting, excessive wetness of the eyelid and eyelashes. Symptoms could start as early as a few months after birth. If left untreated the hairs on the eyelid will touch and rub on the cornea. This can be very painful and could lead to deep corneal ulcers and scarring of the eye and could lead to loss of vision or complete blindness. The diagnosis is made after a thorough eye exam. The veterinarian may also stain the eye to detect corneal ulcers from the eyelashes rubbing on the eye.

Entropion is treatable with early detection and surgical correction. Any dog could have an entropion. It is believed to be an inherited trait. It is often seen in the Shar-Pei, Chow Chow, Spaniels, English Bulldogs, and St. Bernard's. If you are considering a breed in the higher risk category for entropion consult an ophthalmologist about early examination. Also find out from your breeder if any of their dogs have had entropions. To decrease the incidence of entropion, it is recommended that dogs with inherited entropion not be bred. The Canine Eye Registration publishes a list for breed specific recommendations for purebred dogs with entropions.

Keratoconjunctivitis is the medical term for dry eye. The lachrymal gland produces secretions that form tear production. The purpose of these tears is to cleanse and lubricate the cornea. A lack of tear production can cause chronic drying, irritation, and inflammation. A decrease in tear production resulting in drying and inflammation of the cornea and conjunctiva and can lead to blindness if left untreated. Dogs that are symptomatic may have one or more of the following symptoms: eye rubbing, sensitivity to light and squinting. They may also have redness of the eye along with inflammation. A thick yellow mucoid discharge is often associated with dry eye. The cornea itself might appear to be dry.

The cause of keratoconjuctivitis is believed to be immune mediated. The prognosis is good with early treatment. An ophthalmologist can diagnosis dry eye by measuring your dog's tear production. The Schirmer's Tear Test can be done at the ophthalmologist's office. A small strip of paper is placed below the lower eyelid. The strip will absorb the tears and will detect an inadequate level of tear production.

Some breeds are predisposed to dry eye. The Bloodhound, Boston Terrier, Bull Terriers, English Bulldogs, Pekingese, Pugs, Cocker Spaniels, West Highland Terriers and Yorkshire Terriers.

Nictitans Gland Prolapse is often referred to as cherry eye. The gland of the third eyelid comes out of its normal position. The cause of cherry eye is unknown. It is believed to be related to a weakening of the ligamentous attachment of the gland.

Breeds that are predisposed to cherry eye include the Beagle, Bloodhound, English Bulldog and Newfoundland. The diagnosis is made on visual examination of the eye and the treatment is surgical replacement of the gland. If left untreated the prolapse will impair your dog's vision.

Eptopic Cilia are small hairs that grow through the eyelid and rub on the surface of the cornea. It can be a single hair or multiple hairs. Once the hair has formed on the base of one of the glands of the eyelid it will continue to grow. Once it has migrated through the eyelid it will rest and rub on the cornea. Eyelashes rubbing on the cornea are painful. Signs of eptopic cilia include squinting, increase in tear production, rubbing of the eye and the exposure of the third eyelid.

Diagnosis is made on eye exam. A slit lamp biomicroscope will allow your veterinarian to see fine little eyelashes. If left untreated eptopic cilia can cause painful corneal ulcers and may lead to partial or complete vision loss.

Any breed can have eptopic cilia, but it is more prevalent in English Bulldogs, Pugs, and Boston Terriers

The cornea is the transparent part of the eye that covers the anterior chamber. The cornea bends incoming light and focuses it onto the retina in the back of the eye. The cornea is made up of three layers- the epithelium, the stroma and the endotheilium. The cornea has nerve endings that are sensitive and will respond to touch by involuntarily closing the eye. Due to the need for transparency, there are no blood vessels within the cornea. The cornea is continuously nourished with fluid from the aqueous humor, located in the anterior chamber of the eye. Any disruption of its transparency, affects vision. The cornea should be smooth and should have no interruption of its surface. Examples of diseases of the Cornea include:

- Corneal Dystrophy
- Pannus
- Corneal Ulceration

Corneal Dystrophy is an inherited non- inflammatory abnormality of the cornea appearing in both eyes. Opacity forms in the layers of the cornea causing it to have a gray-white appearance and are most often symmetrical. The opacity causes one or more layers of the cornea to lose its clarity. Corneal Dystrophy can lead to blindness if it affects the deep layers of the cornea. Dogs that are at higher risk for corneal dystrophy are Huskys, Beagles, Shelties, Airedales, Bichons and Boston Terriers. It is recommended that dogs with this disease not be bred.

Pannus is an immune mediated corneal disease and is often seen in German Shepherds. Pannus is a chronic inflammation of the surface of the cornea. It often begins as a red vascularized pigment and will gradually spread across the surface of the eye. As the disease progresses the surface of the cornea can become thickened and rough. As the inflammation spreads across the cornea the vision is affected and continues to worsen. If left untreated, it could lead to blindness.

Corneal ulceration. The cornea has several layers. The outermost layer is the epithelium. A corneal ulcer is a hole in the epithelium exposing the inner layers of the cornea. Corneal ulcer can be caused by infection, chronic dry eye, trauma, ingrown hairs or eyelashes. The cornea has a rich nerve supply and a corneal ulcer can be very painful and can cause permanent vision loss. Corneal ulceration should be treated as soon as possible. Symptoms include squinting, pawing or rubbing of the eye, cloudiness or discharge. Diagnosis can be made with flourescent stain testing. The staining will expose the size and location of the ulcer. Other tests may be performed to determine the cause of ulceration.

The Sclera is the white part of a dog's eye. The sclera is a protective layer of the eye and is made up of dense fibrous tissue. The sclera also maintains the shape of the globe. The sclera of your dog's eye should be white and will have small blood vessels running across its surface.

An example of a condition of the sclera includes:

- Scleritis

Scleritis is an inflammatory condition of the sclera, symptoms including redness in the white part of the eye, squinting and tearing. The cause of scleritis can be related to immune mediated diseases or a parasitic disease such as toxoplasmosis but can also be associated with a tick-borne disease, viral or bacterial infection. Cocker Spaniels are in the higher risk category for scleritis. Diagnosis can be made after eye examination.

The Aqueous Humor is a clear watery fluid chamber located in the anterior portion of the eye. Its purpose is to nourish the cornea, maintain intraocular pressure, and carry away waste products. The aqueous humor is continually producing and continually draining fluid. Any obstruction in its ability to drain will lead to increased ocular pressure. One of the most common diseases involving the aqueous humor is glaucoma.

Glaucoma is a buildup of intraocular fluid caused by increased production of fluid or a decrease in the ability to drain fluid. The increase causes pressure to build within the eye. In a normal eye the aqueous humor will drain out of the eye. Symptoms of glaucoma include redness, cloudiness, vision loss, and pain.

A dog with Glaucoma may have an abnormality in the filtering system that allows the eye to drain. Increase in pressure can actually cause the eye to stretch. Dogs can have one of two types of glaucoma primary or secondary.

Dogs with primary glaucoma have an inherited condition. This is seen in breeds such as Cocker Spaniel, Shar Peis, Labradors and Basset Hounds. Secondary glaucoma occurs as a result of other diseases of the eye. It is important to determine which type of glaucoma your dog has, as the treatments may vary. Glaucoma can be diagnosed by a veterinary ophthalmologist.

The uvea consists of three structures the iris, the ciliary body and the choroid. The iris and the ciliary body are the front part of the uvea and the choroid is the back part of the uvea.

The iris is the colored part of the eye that sits behind the cornea. The iris controls the amount of light entering the eye by adjusting the size of the pupil. The ciliary body lies behind the iris. The ciliary body releases aqueous humor to nourish the cornea. The ciliary body has muscle fibers called suspensory ligaments that suspend and adjust the lens to allow the eye to focus on an object. The choroid contains layers of blood vessels that supply blood to the retina.

Some diseases of the Uvea include:

- Hyphema
- Uveitis
- Chorioretinitis

Hyphema occurs when blood leaks into the anterior chamber of the eye. Bleeding occurs when vessels in the iris leak. The blood pools between the cornea and the iris decreasing vision. The leaking can be mild to severe. Blood could also come from behind the iris. Severe untreated hyphema can cause blindness.

There are multiple causes of hyphema such as, hypertension, infection, chronic glaucoma, or a severe blunt trauma to the head. The signs of hyphema are redness within the eye, squinting and decreased vision. Hyphema can be diagnosed by a full eye exam. Your veterinarian may also want to check your dog's blood pressure and blood work to check your dog for any blood clotting diseases.

Uveitis refers to an inflammatory process that involves the anterior portion of the eye. There are many things that can cause anterior uveitis such as infection, immune mediated diseases, trauma, or cancer. The cause may also be unknown or "idiopathic." Symptoms of uveitis include redness, tearing, squinting or a cloudiness of the eye. A dog may also paw or rub at their face.

Diagnosis of uveitis will require a full eye exam with ophthalmoscope. Tonometry tests the pressure of the eye and staining to check for ulceration. Your veterinarian may also want to do blood work. Anterior uveititis can also be a symptom of other diseases and it is important to your dog's treatment to rule out any underlying causes. If left untreated it can result in permanent vision loss.

Chorioretinitis is an inflammation of the chorioid and the retina. The cause of chorioretinits can be viral, bacterial, genetic, parasitic or even unknown cause. It is often seen in animal with toxoplasmosis. A diagnosis can be made after a thorough eye exam with an ophthalmoscope. Dogs with immune mediated disease may be at higher risk.

The pupil is the opening in the iris. The pupil determines the amount of light that enters the eye by making it larger to allow more light and smaller to let in less light. The size of the pupil is controlled by the ciliary muscles. Conditions of the pupil include: Anisocoria

Anisocoria presents as unequal pupil size. One pupil will be larger than the other. The cause of anisocoria can be trauma or disease related. Dogs that suffer significant head injuries such as being hit by a car can present with anisocoria, cancer, glaucoma, and uveitis can also cause anisororia. Treatment is dependent upon the cause.

The Lens is a clear structure that focuses light rays onto the retina. Examples of some of the diseases of the lens include the following:

- Cataract
- Lens Luxation
- Nuclear Sclerosis

Cataracts are a breakdown of the mechanism of the lens fiber. Increased water and insoluble proteins block the clarity of the lens. The eye may appear to have a grayish-blue appearance. Cataracts affect all different types of dogs at different ages. Congenital cataracts can be present at birth, usually in both eyes. The cause could be inherited, from an infection or a toxin in utero. Developmental cataracts will develop early in life and could also be inherited. Other causes include diabetes mellitus, infection, or toxins. Senile cataracts occur later in life usually over the age of six. The diagnosis is made after a thorough eye exam.

Dogs at higher risk for inherited cataracts include Afghan Hounds, Cocker Spaniels, Chesapeake Bay Retrievers, German Shepherds, Golden Retrievers, Labrador Retrievers, and Miniature Schnauzers, Old English Sheepdogs, Standard Poodles, West Highland Terriers and Boston Terriers.

Lens Luxation occurs when the lens dislocates within the eye. The lens lies between the iris and the vitreous humor and is held by suspensory ligaments. A breakdown in the structure of the ligaments can cause a partial or complete dislocation of the lens. Suspensory ligaments breakdown the lens and could fall in the anterior or posterior part of the eye. Symptoms can include discoloration of the eye, pain or squinting

Lens luxation can occur as an inherited disease or secondary to another disease such as glaucoma or trauma. Diagnosis can be made by examining the eye with a slit lamp to closely exam the structures of the eye and determine the location of the lens and inflammation of the other structures of the eye. Dogs at higher risk of inherited lens luxation are in the terrier breeds. It is recommended that dogs with inherited lens luxation not be bred.

Nuclear Sclerosi is one of the most common diseases of the canine lens and is often seen in geriatric dogs. As your dog ages, the center of the lens may become dense and it may appear to the owner that the dog has a grayish blue color to the eye. The age of onset for dogs with nuclear sclerosis is about seven and the lens will continue to harden as the dog ages. This usually occurs in both eyes. The eyes can also appear to be cloudy and may look similar to a dog that has cataracts. Fortunately, a dog's vision is not significantly affected by nuclear sclerosis. A veterinarian upon examination can make diagnosis of nuclear sclerosis. Any breed of dog can have nuclear sclerosis and currently there is no treatment. Owners should be diligent in watching their dog for any vision changes and report them to your veterinarian.

The Victerous Humor is a jelly like substance in the posterior portion of the eye. This jelly like substance maintains the round shape of the eye. Light entering the eye is transmitted through the victreous to the retina. Diseases of the victerous humor include:

- Asteroid Hyalosis

Asteroid Hyalosis is a degenerative disorder of the victerous humor. Small white bodies of calcium and phospholipids form in the vitreous giving the appearance of stars or asteroids. It is most often seen in older dogs and occurs spontaneously. Fortunately, vision is not affected. Asteroid Hyalosis can also be associated with chronic inflammatory diseases of the eye. Diagnosis can be made with an ophthalmic exam.

The Retina is located in the back of the eye and is lined with photoreceptors. Photoreceptors are nerve cells that respond to light. The retina has two types of photoreceptors, rods and cones. Examples of diseases of the retina include:

- Progressive Retinal Degeneration
- Retinal Detachment
- Retinal Dysplasia
- SARD

Progressive retinal degeneration or progressive retinal atrophy (PRD or PRA), is an inherited disease and has several forms. Dogs develop rods and cones in the retina after birth. Some dogs will have an abnormal development or dysplasia, while other dogs may have a slow progressive degeneration of the photoreceptors of the retina. PRD/ PRA affects both eyes. Photoreceptors convert light into electrical signals and as they deteriorate, light will not be able to reach the retina. Dogs that have retinal dysplasia never have proper development of the photoreceptors, and therefore, go blind much more rapidly, usually by the age of one. While dogs that have a progressive degeneration will progress slower, the end result is still the same. Initial symptoms for a dog with PDA/ PDR would start with hesitation in dim lighting. Rods are more affected than cones and they are responsible for vision in low light. Eventually the cones are affected as well and the animal will become blind.

Diagnosis of PDA/PDR starts with a full eye exam from your ophthalmologist. Confirmation of the disease can be determined by performing an electroretinogram. Prevention is the key to this disease, so dogs with this diagnosis should not be bred.

Retinal Detachment is when the retina is lifted or pulled off from its normal position and detaches from the underlying support tissue interrupting a visual message to the optic nerve. Retinal detachment is often the result of other underlying disease and can happen in one or both eyes. Causes of retinal detachment are inherited eye disease, infections, immune mediated diseases, cancer, trauma, or poisoning. Collies are at higher risk for inherited diseases that can cause retinal detachment. Dogs with hypertension are also at higher risk for retinal detachment. Blood leakage from vessels can develop under the retina putting pressure and separating it from the eye.
Diagnosis is made after a thorough eye exam. Further testing may need to be done to identify any underlying disease.

Retinal Dysplasia is an inherited malformation of the retina. Folds form on the outer layer of the retina causing the malformation. Large areas of dysplasia may lead to a loss of vision. In some cases, retinal dysplasia can result in retinal detachment and permanent vision loss. Beagles, Labrador

Retrievers Rottweilers, Cocker Spaniels and Cavalier King Charles Spaniels are at higher risk of retinal dysplasia. It is recommended that dogs with this disease not be bred since it is believed to be a congenital malformation.

SARD stands for Sudden Acquired Retinal Degeneration, and it involves an acute breakdown of the cells of the rods and cones of the retina. SARD was discovered in the 1980's. A dog with SARD will have sudden and complete blindness. Its cause is unknown. Dogs with SARD will have dilated pupils and loss of papillary light reflex (the reflex that controls the diameter of the pupil.) Initially the retina may not show changes on examination. Over time the layers of the retina will continue to degenerate and the retina will have the appearance of retinal atrophy. Electroretinography will give a definitive diagnosis. Currently there is no treatment for SARD. Any dog can be at risk. Dogs with Cushing's disease may be at higher risk.

The Optic Nerve is located in the back of the eye. It is a very important function as it relays visual nerve impulse to the brain. Diseases of the optic nerve include:

- Optic Neuritis.

Optic Neuritis is an inflammation of the optic nerve. Each eye has an optic nerve. The nerve is in the back of the eye and leads to the brain. Optic neuritis can have many causes-viral, immune mediated, tick borne or inflammation of the brain or retina. In some cases, we do not know the cause. In those patients, we determine the cause to be "idiopathic" or of unknown causes. Optic neuritis can lead to blindness and can occur in any breed. Symptoms of optic neuritis are dependent upon the cause. Sometimes there are no symptoms other than blindness.

The Brain is the organ that is responsible for vision. As I have discussed previously the eye is really a tool that the brain uses to see the world. I have included it in this book because there are several diseases of the brain that can cause partial or total blindness. Some of the diseases include:

- Encephalitis
- Granulomatous Meningoencephalitis
- Hepatic Encephalopathy
- Hydrocephalus
- Hypoxia
- Tumors
- Severe head trauma

Encephalitis is an inflammatory disease of the central nervous system which includes the brain and the spinal cord. Causes of encephalitis can be viral, bacterial, fungal, tick borne or idiopathic. Diagnosis can be made with an MRI and a spinal tap. Dogs that have encephalitis will have an increase in white blood cells in their spinal fluid. Symptoms of encephalitis include blindness, seizures, walking in circles and lack of co-ordination or staggering. Pugs are at higher risk for encephalitis.

Granulomatous Meningoencephalitis (GME) is an inflammatory disease that affects the central nervous system, causing neurological symptoms including sudden blindness. GME can present as focal, multifocal or as an ocular manifestation. Diagnosis is made on physical exam, MRI of the brain and spinal cord, and analysis of cerebrospinal fluid. Typically, GME affects small breed dogs and usually occurs around middle age.

Hepatic encephalopathy is a degenerative brain disease. The causes of this are related to liver disease. Some dogs have congenital liver disease or shunts where blood is diverted around the liver. Dogs that do not have a congenital liver disease can develop one later in life from toxic or infectious diseases. The liver converts ammonia into urea. When it is not able to do so, high levels of ammonia will circulate through the bloodstream to the brain. Hepatic encephalopathy will cause symptoms such as abnormal behavior, circling, head pressing, and blindness. Diagnosis of hepatic encephalopathy can be made by your veterinarian with blood work to check ammonia levels and bile acid testing.

Hydrocephalus is an accumulation of the cerebrospinal fluid in the brain. The most common form of hydrocephalus is congenital. It occurs less frequently in adult dogs and is often related to tumor or an infection that obstructs the pathway of the cerebrospinal fluid. Hydrocephalus can be diagnosed with a CAT scan or MRI. Your vet may also take skull radiographs or ultrasound the brain if there is an open fontanel.

Hydrocephalus is most common in small and toy breed dogs such as Chihuahuas and Yorkshire Terriers

Hypoxia is an inadequate amount of oxygen supply to the brain. Some puppies are blind at birth from an inadequate amount of oxygen to the brain during delivery. Hypoxia can result in permanent and irreversible brain damage and can occur in any breed.

Tumors can be present in the brain. The symptoms of a dog with a brain tumor will vary depending on where the tumor is in the brain. Behavior changes, blindness and seizures are the most common of symptoms.

Brain tumors are diagnosis with MRI or CAT scans. Treatments may include surgery, radiation or chemotherapy, and should be treated by an oncologist. Boxers and Boston Terriers are at higher risk for pituitary tumors, and

Dobermans and Golden Retrievers are at a higher risk for meningiomas. However, any breed can present with a brain tumor.

Traumatic head injury can lead to severe brain dysfunction including blindness due to swelling or hemorrhage. The optic nerve can also be torn away from the eye. It would take a significant trauma for this to occur. The diagnosis of brain injury can be determined by CAT scan or MRI. Dogs who are not properly restrained on a leash or in the yard are at higher risk for being hit by cars and therefore, are at higher risk for head trauma. Treatment for head injury does vary depending on the severity. Severe trauma can also cause the dislocation of the eye called proptosis, and may require removal of the eye.

If you believe your dog has any problems with the structures of the eye, contact your veterinarian or veterinary ophthalmologist immediately.

Acknowledgements:

Internet Resources

www.ahvma.org The American Holistic Veterinary Medical Association.

www.anglevest.homestead.com An assist aid for blind dogs.

www.aspca.org American Society for Prevention of Cruelty of Animals Reading Canine Body Posture Canine Animal Care.

www.avco.org/locate.htm Locate an ophthalmologist in your state.

www.blinddogs.com/ A site for owners of low vision and blind dogs.

www.blinddogguide.com Receive a free copy of The Blind Dog Guide.

www.blinddog.info A forum for discussion of blind dog issues.

www.blinddogs.net/ A site for sharing stories of blind dogs and informational links.

www.deltasociety.org/ Improving human health through services and therapy animals.

www.doggles.com Protective eyewear for dogs.

www.handicappedpets.com Resource for owners with disabled dogs.

www.kindredspiritkindredcare.com Making Health Decisions on Behalf of our Animal Companions.

www.ocuglo.com Natural canine vision supplements.

www.petplace.com Blindness in Dogs Dr. Noelle Mcnabb and Separation Anxiety by Dr. Alice Moon Panelli

www.throughadogsears.com Using music to improve the lives of dogs and their people.

www.veterianrypartner.com First Aid and Emergency Care Gfeller, Roger W. DipAcvecc, Thomas, Michael W. and Mayo, Isaac a VIN company.

www.vmdb.org/cer.html The Canine Eye Registration Foundation.

www.whole-dog-journal.com/

WWW.blinddogtraining.com
Miki Saito, CPDT-KA Yokohama, Japan

References Books:

Barlough Jeffery E. *UC Davis Book of Dogs a Complete Medical Reference Guide for Dogs and Puppies.* HarperCollins 1995

Barnett, KC. Samsom, Jane. and Heinrick Christine. *Canine Ophthalmology an Atlas and Text.* Harcourt Publishers, Elsevier Science 2002

Bockstahler, Barbara, Levine, David and Millis, Darryl. *Essential Facts of Physiotherapy in Dogs and Cats.* Babenhausen-Germany: Die Deutsche Bibliothek 2004

Cargill, Marie. *Acupuncture a Viable Medical Alternative.* Connecticut: Praeger Publishers 1994

Dodman, Nicholas H. *Best Behavior Unleashing Your Dog's Instinct to Obey.* Massachusetts: Good Dog Library2004

Gelatt, Kirk N. *Color Atlas of Veterinary Ophthalmology* Blackwell Publishing 2001

Horowitz, Alexandra. *Inside of a Dog What Dogs See, Smell and Know.* New York: Scribner 2009

Levin, Caroline D. *Living with Blind Dogs A resource Book and Training Guide for the Owners of Blind and Low Vision Dogs.* Oregon: Lantern Publications 1998

Maggs, David J. Miller, Paul E. and Ofri, Ron. *Slatters Fundamental Veterinary Ophthalmology Fourth Edition* Missouri: Saunders Elsevier 2008

Mcelroy Chernak, Susan. *Animals as Teachers and Healers.* New York: The Ballantine Publishing Group 1996

McMillan, Franklin D. *Mental Health and Well-Being in Animals.* Iowa: Blackwell Publishing Professional 2005

Nakaya, Shannon F. *Kindred Spirit, Kindred Care: Making Health Decisions on Behalf of Our Animal Companions.* California: New World Library 2005

Parsons, Emma. *Click to Calm Healing the Aggressive Dog.*

Massachusetts: Sunshine Books 2004

Tilman, Peggy. *Clicking with Your Dog Step by Step in Pictures.* Massachusetts: Sunshine Books 2001

Villalobos, Alice. DVM. Kaplan, Laurie. Canine and Feline Geriatric Oncology. Quality of life scale adapted from Villalobao, A. E

Articles:
Akyol-Salman T. "Effects of autologous serum eye drops on corneal wound healing after superficial keratectomy in rabbits"

Brooks, Wendy C. DVM "Enucleation (Removal of the Eye)" The Pet Health Library DipABVP Education Director VeterinaryPartner.com

Graham L, Wells DL, and Hepper PG, "The Influence of Olfactory Stimulation on the Behavior of Dogs Housed in Rescue Shelter" Applied Animal Behavior Science 2005; 91: 143-153

Grandin, Temple Ph.D. "Calming Effects of Deep Touch Pressure in Patients with Autistic Disorder, College Students, and Animal" Journal of Child and Adolescent Psychopharmacology Vol 2, Number 1, 1992

"Gene discovery could lead to better understanding of how retinal cells regenerate" Dec 1, 2011 DVM NEWSMAGAZINE

"Healing Touch Therapy Alternative Therapies Relax Heart Patients" Harvard Heart Letter October 2005; 16 (2):3

Kidd, Randy DVM PHD "The Canine Sense of Smell" The Whole Dog Journal issues 7-11

Komiva, M. Sugiyama, A. Tanabe K.. Uchino, T. Takeuchi, T. "Evaluation of the effect of topical application of lavender oil on autonomic nerve activity in dogs" AJVR Vol 70 No 6 June 2009

Mandsager R. DVM "What do Dogs See"? A Review of Paul E. Miller and Christopher J. Murphy's "Vision in Dogs"

McCrave EA "Diagnostic Criteria for Separation Anxiety in the Dog" Vet Clinic of North America Small Animal Practice 1991 21 (2) 247-255

McGreevy P. Grassi TD; Harman A.M "A Strong Correlation Exist Between the distribution of the Retinal Ganglia Cells and Nose Length in the Dog". Brain, Behavior, and Evoution 2004 63:13-22

Miller, Paul E. Murphy, Christopher "Vision in Dogs" Veterinary Medical Associates JAVMA vol 207 no 12 pp. 1623-1634 December 15, 1995

Miller Paul E. "Vision in Animals what do Dogs and Cats See"? Waltham OSU Symposium Small Animal Ophthalmology 2001

Neitz, Jay. Geist, Timothy. and Jacobs Gerlald H. "Color Vision in Dogs" Visual Neuroscience 3: 119-125 1989

Nietz, Jay. Carroll, Joseph. And Neitz, Maureen "Color Vision Almost Reason Enough for Having Eyes" Optic and Photonics News January 2001 Optical Society of America

Pageat, Patrick. CEVA Santé Animal study done in November 1999 and November 2000 clinical trials

Probst, Sarah "Through the Eyes of Your Canine" University of Illinois College of Veterinary Medicine online source **www.vetmed.illnois.edu/petcolumns** Pet Column June 15th 1998

Ryan, Kirk DVM, Marks Steven L. BVSc, Dacvim, Kerwin, Sharon C. DVM MS DACVS "Granulomatous Meningoencphalomelitis in Dogs" Louisana State University Science Daily (2007)

Schachner, Adena. Brady, Timothy F. Pepperberg, Irene M. Haucer, Mark C "Spontaneous Motor Entrainment to Music in Vocal Mimicking Species" Current Biology volume 19 issue 10 831-836 April 2009

Wagner, S et al. Bioacoustic Research & Development Canine Research Summary 2004

Wang SM, Kain ZN Auricular "Acupuncture A potential Treatment for Anxiety Anesthesia and Analgesia" Feb 2001; 92 (2) 548-553

Wells, Debroah "Aromatherapy Travel Induced Excitement in Dogs" Journal of American Veterinary Medical Association September 15 2006 Vol 229 No. 6 pg 964-967

Well D.L. "The Influence of Auditory Stimulation on the Behavior in Dogs Housed in Rescue Shelter" Animal Welfare 11 2002 385-393 (Studies on the Auditory Stimulation on the Behavior of Dogs Housed in Rescue Shelter) Animal Welfare 11 2002 385-393

Sources:

Department of Ophthalmology, Atatürk University Faculty of Medicine, Erzurum, Turkey. **ilkakyol@atauni.edu.tr**

Maire Hopfensperger DVM American College of Veterinary Behaviorists specialty training program;
American Veterinary Society of Animal Behavior;
American Veterinary Medical AssociationMichigan State University:
Enhancing the Canine and Feline Veterinary Experience.

Miko Satio blinddogtraing.com

http://www.dogtrainingnation.com/how-to-train-a-dog/how-to-teach-your-dog-chin-rests/

McGowan RT, Rehn T, Norling Y, & Keeling LJ (2014). Positive affect and learning: exploring the "Eureka Effect" in dogs. *Animal cognition, 17* (3), 577-87 PMID: **24096703**

http://myspecialneedsdogs.com/commands-blind-puppy/

http://www.patriciamcconnell.com/lets-talk-considering-another-dog

https://learningfromdogs.com/tag/amygdala/

Made in the USA
San Bernardino, CA
25 September 2018